Focusing On...

Gebruder Heubach Dolls

The Art of Gebruder Heubach: Dolls and Figurines

by Jan Foulke

photographs by Howard Foulke

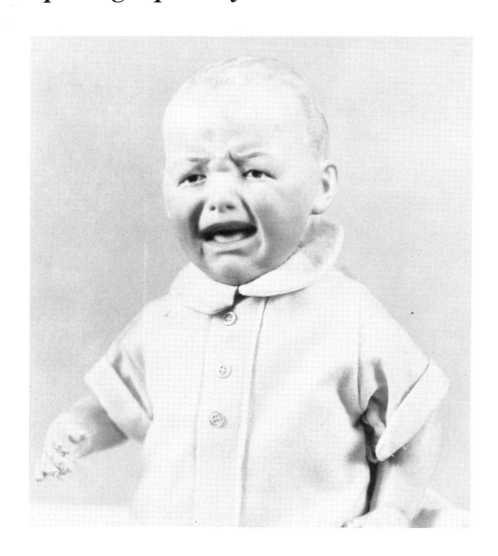

Published By 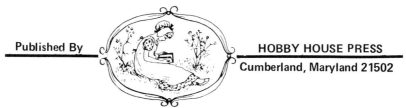 HOBBY HOUSE PRESS

Cumberland, Maryland 21502

Front Cover: Left to right: 15in (38.1cm) pouty with mold number 6969 discussed in detail on page 13 (Illustration 8). 7in (17.8cm) wigged "Bonnie Babe" incised 1393 discussed on page 35 (Illustration 63). 8in (20.3cm) wigged "Bonnie Babe" impressed with the Heubach square mark and number 12386 discussed on page 35 (Illustration 64). Mechanical "Whistling Jim" discussed on page 39 (Illustration 70). 15in (38.1cm) pouty with mold number 6969 discussed on page 13 (Illustration 9).

Back Cover: TOP: One of the most spectacular Heubach pieces with babies in this bisque basket trinket box with a removable lid. The woven basket is tinted a natural straw color with the top edge, basket rim and clasps and hinges in a darker brown. Four blonde haired babies peek over the rim of the basket. BOTTOM: 14in (35.6cm) Heubach googlie discussed on page 41 (Illustration 71).

Title Page Photograph: This crying baby, obviously quite unhappy, is a very rare and desirable Heubach character doll. He is 17in (43.2cm) tall and incised only Germany in the Heubach manner. He has molded and brush-stroked hair, intaglio eyes and a look of pure anguish. *Ruth Noden Collection.*

ISBN: 0-87588-148-3

Acknowledgement

Many thanks to the collectors who allowed their dolls to be photographed for this book: Ruby Arnold, Dottie Baer, Rosemary Dent, Mary Goolsby, Gail Hiatt, Violet Mackemull, Sheila Needle, Ruth Noden, Mary Lou Rubright, Jilda Sallade, Shila Vanderwalt, Mike White and Richard Wright. They have enriched our hobby by their willingness to share their dolls and information with other interested collectors.

Table of Contents

Frontispiece 4
Introduction 7
Gebruder Heubach Marks 8
Index of Mold Numbers 8
Background 10
The Art of Heubach 11
The Pouties 13
Smiling Children 25
Mechanical Dolls 37
Googlies 41
Traditional Styles 44
Christmas Novelties 47
All-Bisque Characters 49
Position Babies 52, 56
Action Figures 54
Easter Bunnies 55
Piano Babies 58
Child Figures 60

Frontispiece

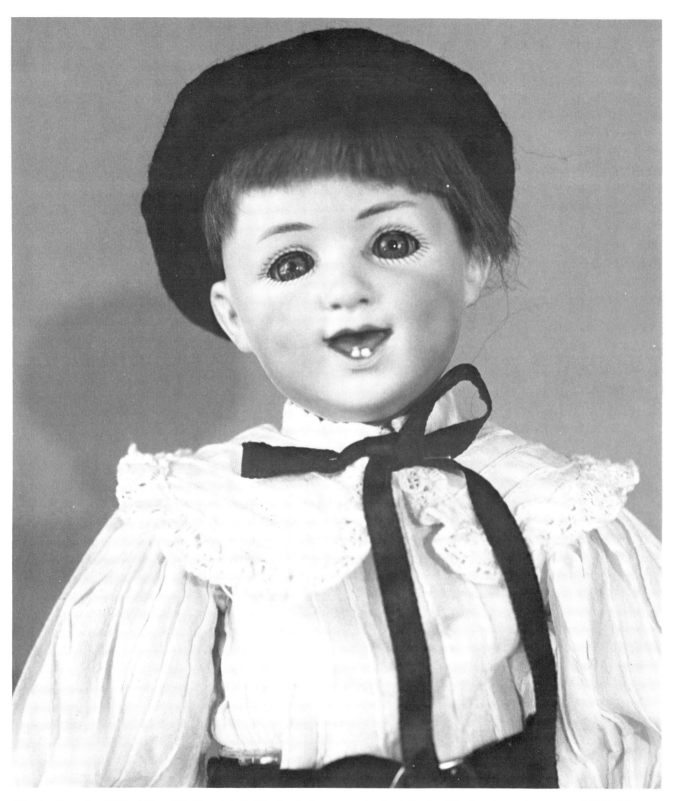

Illustration 1. This 13in (33.0cm) tall Heubach boy marked with the Heubach sunburst and 5636 is possibly one of "The Smiling 'Jubilee' Babies" advertised in the January 1909 *Playthings* by Strobel and Wilken, a company which distributed German bisque dolls. These dolls had jointed composition child bodies, not baby bodies. *Mary Lou Rubright Collection.*

Introduction

The factory of Gebruder Heubach is on record as having been established in 1820. The Heubach family apparently was quite large, and several other branches were also involved in porcelain making. The Gebruder Heubach factory at Lichte, Thuringia, Germany, made china tableware, novelties and figurines as well as dolls. They probably made china head dolls and later the bisque lady dolls with the molded fancy hairstyles and the beautifully decorated shoulder plates. However, this is conjecture as these types of dolls are never marked with a factory name.

It is fairly easy to trace the development of doll styles of most companies making bisque dolls, but the dolls of Gebruder Heubach are much more difficult to classify. Most of the older factories follow logically through the stages of the closed-mouth child dolls, the open-mouth child dolls and then the character dolls. Although Gebruder Heubach was presumably making dolls though all of these periods also, and indeed had doll agents, still it is puzzling as to what dolls he was producing before the early 1900s. It seems as though he

RIGHT: Illustration 2. Not a beautiful doll by any means, but certainly one of the outstanding character faces created by the Heubach brothers is this rare American Indian doll. The face is similar to the many paintings of Indians which were done by the frontier painters and were so popular in the United States. It is lined with worry and care, and the brows are furrowed. The eyelids are heavy with age; the nose is broad. The mouth is turned down, probably toothless. Her wig is done in gray mohair braids over a solid dome head. As the original leather clothes had rotted, this squaw was re-dressed by the Sioux Indians in 1950 in a copy of an 1891 war dress worn by that tribe. This shoulder head doll is on a body of cloth with composition arms and legs. She is incised with a square mark and 8457. An Indian chief, a companion doll to her, can be seen in the color section. Chief. *Richard Wright Collection.* Squaw. *Ruth Noden Collection.*

Sample Heubach markings

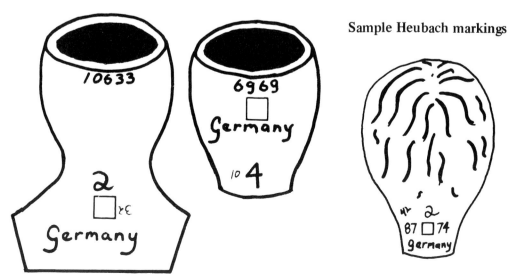

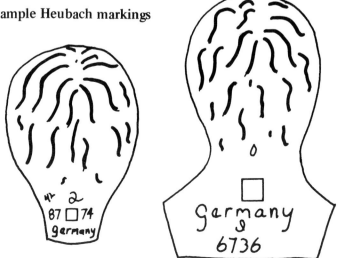

specialized in the production of character dolls, and they did not come on the market until about 1909. Even if he were making character dolls by the early 1900s, as he might have been, this leaves a great gap in our knowledge of what bisque dolls Heubach made from 1880 until 1900.

Even the mold numbers seem to be of little help in this problem. Some companies, for instance Simon & Halbig, used a fairly consistent numbering system. At least the mold numbers were in chronological order. But I have not yet figured out the Gebruder Heubach system. Possibly the five-digit mold numbers are the last dolls that were made, however. The googlies, which are known to be later dolls, have high four-digit numbers. Further study of the Heubach mold numbers is definitely indicated. Working on the Heubach mold numbers has been a most frustrating task since the numbers are small and lightly impressed which often makes them very difficult to decipher. The 3s, 6s and 8s are very confusing; 0s and 9s are particularly bad. The number usually consists of four digits, scmetimes five. Sometimes part of the number does not even stamp. On open crown dolls, the mold number is usually high at the crown opening, often covered by glue from the wig; on shoulder head dolls with molded hair, it is usually down at the bottom of the shoulder covered by the body. On socket dolls with molded hair, it is usually divided into two parts, with two numbers on each side of the square mark. Beside the mold numbers, there are also occasionally two other numbers sometimes upside down impressed together, some numbers stamped in green and possibly a size number as well. These mold numbers have been recorded as accurately as possible, but there is still some possibility of error. Perhaps with careful tabulation, these numbers will yet get sorted out. This book is actually just the beginning of our work with Heubachs and we will continue collecting photographs and numbers of dolls not in this book.

Another problem in classification arises when some of the dolls have no mold numbers at all, simply a square mark or a sunburst. Then there are a few obviously Heubach dolls which are marked only Germany. Also some do not have the trademark, only the mold number. Evidently the factory was not thinking in terms of convenience for collectors 100 years down the road!

Gebruder Heubach Marks

Incised

Square Mark

Sunburst

Stamped in green, red or blue

Germany

Also in addition to the mold number and trademark

Incised

D   meaning unknown

$\frac{5}{0}$ fraction or whole number probably denotes size

I2   one or two numbers, sometimes upside down

Stamped

9   single or double green number, often blurred

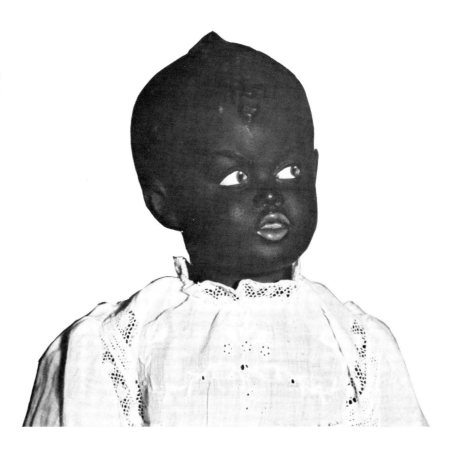

Illustration 3. Very rare among Heubach dolls are the black characters. Only occasionally is one found. This doll could be treated as a boy or girl. The black molded hair is short and given a fuzzy look. The dark eyes are deeply incised with painted highlights, and, of course, the whites are very outstanding in the very dark black face. Her eyebrows are molded as are her upper and lower eyelids. Her pink lips are thick and slightly parted as though ready to speak to whoever is calling her name. She is 19in (48.3cm) tall on a very good black jointed composition body. She is incised with a sunburst and 6, possibly a size number. Unfortunately there is no mold number on her, but an identical doll has been recorded as mold No. 7671. *Old Curiosity Shop.*

Index of Mold Numbers

Index of mold numbers on doll heads shown in this book, not including all-bisque dolls

5636	— Laughing with glass eyes and wig, socket head	Illustration 48
5777	— Dolly Dimple, socket head	Illustrations 41 & 42
6692	— Pouty shoulder head, intaglio eyes, molded hair	Illustration 31
6736	— Laughing shoulder head, intaglio eyes, molded hair	Illustrations 54 & 67
6897	— Laughing socket head, intaglio eyes, molded hair	Illustration 52
6969	— Pouty, glass eyes, wig, socket head	Illustrations 8, 9 & 10
6970	— Pouty, glass eyes, wig, socket head	Illustrations 11 & 12
7246	— Pouty, glass eyes, wig, socket head	Illustrations 13, 14, 16 & 17
7247	— Pouty, glass eyes, wig, socket head	Illustrations 18 & 19
7248	— Pouty, glass eyes, wig, socket head	Illustration 15
7256	— Pouty, glass eyes, wig, socket head	Illustration 20
7307	— Smiling, intaglio eyes, wig, socket head	Illustration 56
7314	— Laughing, intaglio eyes, molded hair, socket head	Illustration 68
7407	— Pouty, glass eyes, wig, socket head	Illustrations 21 & 22
7602	— Pouty, intaglio eyes, molded hair	Illustration 33
7604	— Smiling, intaglio eyes, molded hair, socket head	Illustrations 53 & 65
7622	— Pouty, intaglio eyes, molded hair, socket head	Illustrations 26, 27 & 28
7671	— Black child	Illustration 3

7711	— Traditional, open mouth, glass eyes, wig	Illustration 83
7763	— Coquette, socket head	Illustration 62
7764	— Girl, molded hair with enameled bow	Illustration 6
7788	— Coquette, socket head	Illustrations 60 & 61
7911 or 7971	— Smiling, molded hair, intaglio eyes, socket head	Illustration 57
7977	— Baby Stuart, socket head	Illustrations 37 & 38
8017	— Pouty, glass eyes, wig, socket head	Illustration 23
8191	— Smiling, molded hair, intaglio eyes, socket head	Illustration 59
8192	— Traditional, open mouth, glass eyes, wig, socket head	Illustrations 89 & 90
8306	— Smiling, molded hair, intaglio eyes, shoulder head	Illustration 58
8316	— Grinning, glass eyes, wig, socket head	Illustrations 46 & 47
8420	— Pouty, glass eyes, wig, socket head	Illustrations 24 & 25
8457	— Indian, shoulder head	Illustration 2
8589	— Googly, intaglio eyes, molded hair, socket	Illustrations 79 & 80
8729	— Googly, molded hair, intaglio eyes, socket head	Illustration 81
8774	— Whistling Jim	Illustration 70
8878	— Pouty, molded hair, intaglio eyes, socket head	Illustration 40
9081	— Googly, painted eyes, molded hair girl, socket head	Illustration 82
9141	— Winking, socket head	Illustrations 74 & 75
9167	— Pouty, molded hair, socket head, intaglio eyes	Illustration 30
9355	— Dolly Dimple, unmarked shoulder head	Illustrations 43 & 44
9573	— Googly, glass eyes, wig, socket head	Illustrations 76 & 77
9578	— Pouty, intaglio eyes, socket head	Illustration 35
10532	— Traditional, open-mouth, wig, glass eyes, socket head	Illustrations 84, 85 & 86
10586	— Traditional, open-mouth, wig, glass eyes, socket head	Illustration 88
10633	— Dolly face	
12386	— Bonnie Babe with wig	Illustration 64

Background

Judging from the known output of the Gebruder Heubach factory, it seems safe to assume that they specialized in the production of character dolls. Their line seems to have included very few of the "dolly-faced" girls which were the dominant production of the other German doll makers. Even after the introduction of the character doll, the "dolly-faced" doll continued to dominate the market in sales as well as production. The character dolls were considered by many people to be innovative and arty, and appealed more to liberal than conservative people who liked to stick by the familiar.

The revolution in character dolls was essentially a German movement. It began in Munich in the early years of the 20th century with a group of designers, the foremost of whom was Marion Kaulitz whose dolls were known as "Munich Art Dolls." These dolls were more real-looking and childlike than the pretty doll-faced dolls of the time which represented an idealized child instead of a real one. Social history is of necessity entwined with the history of toys, as are industrial developments and changes in artistic tastes. It seems that an awakened interest in children as real people in their own right instead of being merely tiny copies of adults had a profound effect upon the design of dolls. The time was ripe for this drastic change, but the success of the character doll was not an overnight happening.

In the February 1908 *Playthings* Samstag and Hilder Brothers advertised "Dolls with the real childlike face. The accomplishment is announced after years of careful experiments and persevering effort . . . . These dolls have been modeled from living subjects under the direction of the most famous artist of Munich, and they represent the very latest development of doll making." The dolls are not pictured, but they could have been the Munich Art Dolls.

The first ad actually picturing bisque character dolls was from the January 1909 *Playthings* where Strobel and Wilken Co. advertised "The Smiling 'Jubilee' Babies," three dolls which appear to be Heubach dolls from mold number 5636 with smiling faces, having the open/closed mouth with two lower teeth, glass eyes and wigs. These dolls, while dressed as babies, are on regular jointed composition bodies. This ad shows that Heubach was early into character dolls, and probably a leader in the field. It is always exciting to make a discovery like this in an area as elusive as the Heubach company. Later in the same issue the "Smiling Doll" is referred to as "hand-modeled to represent—not the ideal type, but the double of many a little girl in real life." And in the same issue George Borgfeldt advertised "dolls with human expressions modeled by well-known artists in Munich from living subjects; boys', girls' and women's faces in a variety of expressions." And so the era of the character doll had arrived in the United States.

In April 1909 Strobel and Wilken ran the first of their ads for the character dolls produced by

ABOVE: Illustration 4. A 16in (40.6cm) pensive-faced Heubach character boy, mold No. 6970, who appears to have been modeled from real life by an artist. *Mike White Collection.*

Kammer and Rinehardt. The bisque heads were actually made by Simon & Halbig, a company which is never mentioned since, like Heubach, they made heads for other producers who put the whole doll together.

In January and February 1910, Strobel and Wilken also advertised "K & R character dolls modeled from living subjects by artists--babies, boys, and girls in a large variety of natural facial expressions."

In February 1910 "Boy dolls with smiling character faces in all styles and prices with hearty, carefree faces" were mentioned. Heubach dolls were doubtless included with these. A store display window of Christmas 1910 shows a case of dolls which appear to be tiny Heubach pouty babies.

In January and February 1911, Louis Lindner & Sons advertised dolls which appear to be Heubachs: two laughing girls, a pouty boy and a pouty baby. These apparently were popular models as they are the most commonly found today. In their October 1914 ad they were still showing characters with laughing faces which appear to be Heubach dolls.

In May 1911 Selchow and Righter advertised dolls from leading European factories. Two which are shown appear to be a Heubach pouty baby with intaglio eyes and molded hair, and the almost unmistakable Heubach crying baby which is shown on the frontispiece.

In 1910 the editorial pages of *Playthings* contained quite a few discussions about the new character dolls, mostly promoting them as an addition to the doll-faced doll, not a replacement for her. Apparently the character dolls were not an instant success, and it took several years for the line to become established. But it never did replace the ever-popular doll-faced doll.

The Art of Heubach

The basis of the art of the Heubach brothers is the ability to create faces in bisque which are believably real. An astounding sidelight is the variety of characters which they produced. Without a doubt it can be said that Heubach specialized in the production of bisque character dolls, many of them quite unusual, and some of them far surpassing the attempts at characterization of other doll makers of that time. Many of the ultimate examples of character dolls are indeed products of the factory of Gebruder Heubach, as evidenced in the countenance of the howling baby used in the frontispiece, as he protests some certain injustice.

The Heads

As will be seen throughout this book, the Heubach brothers produced heads in a wider variety than any other doll maker. Apparently, their intent was to appeal to as broad a market as possible through the wide range of dolls available. Bisque heads were produced in both the socket type, which would be mounted on a jointed composition body, and the shoulder head type with head and shoulders in one piece, which would be mounted on a cloth or kid body. Apparently, Heubach continued to produce the shoulder heads in fairly large quantity far after the time when they were considered old-fashioned by other doll makers. Obviously, there was a market for them or the line would have been dropped. In analyzing the situation, it would seem that the shoulder heads were perhaps cheaper to produce and could be sold as a less expensive line of dolls, especially those which had no need for wigs or inset glass eyes which would, of course, add extra expense. Then probably the cloth bodies were less expensive than the jointed composition bodies which would have involved many more steps to make.

The Bisque

The Heubach bisque is of the highest quality, sanded to a smooth finish. Gebruder Heubach is the only factory known to have sometimes used the pink bisque in the manufacture of its doll heads, although many were also made of standard white bisque. Looking into that head and seeing that pink bisque can be quite shocking if one is not aware of this fact! This was a sensible move, however, as it eliminated one step in the manufacturing process; the head did not have to be given the preliminary coat of flesh color but was simply tinted and fired. Although Heubach did use the pink bisque, his use of it for doll heads is not to be confused with the use of pink bisque for the later all-bisque dolls, which do not have the fired-in tint that the doll heads have.

ABOVE: Illustration 5. This 22in (55.9cm) boy is impressed with mold No. 10532. He has a more traditional-style face with an open-mouth and four upper teeth, possibly a later doll because of the higher mold number and the jointed composition toddler body which was a development of later years of the second decade of the 20th century. *Ruth Noden Collection.*

RIGHT: Illustration 6. Two girl shoulder heads with molded hair. The one on the left is the popular "Coquette," which also was available as a socket head. The one on the right is a quite rare model. She has also been seen as a socket head with the square mark and 7764. *1914 Marshall Field & Company catalog.*

The Decoration

Although sometimes an inferior head appears, for the most part the Heubach dolls are very beautifully decorated. The sometimes inferior ones tend to be small heads which were probably produced in enormous quantities for use not only as dolls, but as novelty items, and perhaps not as great care was given to their production. The flesh tones are pink in contrast to the tones of the early German and French dolls which are white and pale. The cheeks are rosy, as befits a healthy German child. The eyebrows are usually feathered in tiny brush strokes, although sometimes in the smaller and perhaps later dolls only one stroke is used for each eyebrow. The eyelashes are often heavily painted; sometimes none at all or only the upper ones are given to the painted-eye dolls. The mouths are tinted a pleasing color, and the lips are wide or thin, often depending upon the mood of the artist. Seldom is any shading done on the lips. A large number of the Heubach dolls have open/closed mouths where the lips are parted, but there is no actual slit in the bisque. Many of these dolls have molded and/or painted teeth. Some of the Heubach dolls have closed mouths. A few have open mouths with a slit in the bisque to accommodate inset teeth and a tongue if desired.

The Eyes

The Heubach brothers followed the fashion in dolls by using the standard blown glass eyes with weights which would allow the doll to sleep. This was a popular innovation and doll catalogs widely advertised the fact that dolls could be put to sleep by laying them down. However, one eye type was almost uniquely their own, the artistic intaglio eye, of which their artists became masters. Other companies did produce dolls with painted eyes having a round molded eyeball, but Gebruder Heubach was almost alone in making the intaglio eye which had an indented pupil and iris to give the eye more depth.

The Heubach intaglio eye is in itself a work of art. When the eyes are painted, the pupil is usually larger than the iris. Each iris is given a raised white dot highlight which adds to its look of reality. The upper and lower eyelids are molded. A dark line outlines the upper lid; two red dots usually mark the inside corner of the eye. Occasionally upper and lower or only upper eyelashes are added. It is true that perhaps the intaglio eye was cheaper to produce as it was probably easier to simply paint an eye rather than have to cut eyeholes and inset the glass eyes; even then eyelashes would have had to have been painted. But perhaps most important to doll collectors today is the fact that the intaglio eye allowed a wider range of expressions to be produced. In modeling the faces, the artists did not have to be concerned with accommodating a sleeping eye mechanism, and therefore they were allowed much more artistic freedom to create faces with modeling detail around the eyes. Some models were made which could be produced with either intaglio or glass eyes.

The Hair

Probably no other company used the molded hair styles to the extent that the Heubach factory did. This, too, was doubtless considered old-fashioned, and was certainly a throwback to the molded hair dolls of the 1870s. Here again it was a savings as it precluded the purchase of wigs for the dolls. As manufacturers of figurines, the Heubach people were apparently very capable of producing quite lovely molded hair. A look at some of the dolls within this book will prove that point. Very seldom, except sometimes for the babies and the later all-bisque items, were the dolls given bald heads with just painted on hair. Mostly the hair was styled

Illustration 7. Another character in real life style, the so-called "laughing child" mold No. 5636, shown this time as a girl. *Gail Hiatt Collection.*

The Bodies

It has come to be generally accepted that Heubach probably did not make bodies at all. Certainly it is known that Heubach did sell heads to many doll producers and distributors who provided their own bodies for the dolls. This at least accounts for the tremendous range of types of bodies on which Heubach dolls appear. Apparently a great number of socket heads were sold to French producers because many Heubach heads turn up on jointed composition or wooden bodies of French manufacture. Some of the papier-mâché bodies on particularly the smaller dolls are terribly crude. In fact, some are of such a poor quality that it is a wonder that they have not just disintegrated over the years. The torsos are just a tough cardboard, and the arms and legs seem to be just stuck on. Sometimes the whole thing looks put together until one has seen enough of these to know that indeed, as terrible as they are, they are right. Some of the composition bodies are of excellent quality on both babies and children indicating that they are probably top-of-the line dolls. Price consideration would have to be the only explanation for these contrasts.

The shoulder heads also appear on many body types of varying quality. Some of them are pink or white muslin with sometimes undistinguished papier-mâché hands, sometimes nice bisque ones. Other fabric bodies were also used, as were real and imitation kid bodies, again in varying degrees of quality. It is sometimes nearly impossible to determine whether or not a Heubach head is on its original body, as there are so many possibilities. It is a great temptation to transfer some of the lovely heads on very poor bodies to a body which is better in quality! This probably boils down to a question of preserving originality whenever one is sure.

Some of the companies for which Heubach supplied heads are Cuno and Otto Dressel, whose wing mark is found on the backs of excellent quality pink composition bodies carrying Heubach heads with the 6969 mold number. Others known are Gebruder Ohlhaver for whom Heubach made a coquette with his Revalo trademark, Eisenmann & Company for whom they made a googly and Wagner and Zetzsche for whom they made a character baby. Johannes Dietrich who use the Igodi trademark also purchased Heubach heads. There must be others which will someday come to light as more bits and pieces of this puzzle are fit together. However, most companies probably just ordered stock Heubach heads which would carry only the Heubach mark. Several companies could be buying the same head, which again would account for the fact of the same head turning up on several different types of bodies.

realistically with lovely long and short curls, brush strokes around the face to add reality, comb marks throughout the hair to give texture, a crown from which the hair swirled out and sometimes a part. Little girls were often given a molded ribbon or bow.

Among the most sought after Heubachs are those with the molded bonnets. These dolls have wisps of hair sticking out from the sides or bottoms of their bonnets. This was a rare feature tried by only a few companies other than Heubach.

While molded hair was popular with the Heubach designers, they also produced dolls which could be given wigs. Some of their models were made both ways.

Another interesting way Heubach coped with hair was to flock the head. This gave texture and felt fuzzy to the touch, but was not particularly long lasting, and much has worn off by this late date. However, Heubach was not alone in flocking hair; other companies did this also.

As mentioned, some of the small babies and the all-bisque items have bald heads, or nearly bald heads with only a tiny curl or two. The hair on these dolls was achieved by painting, usually with brush marks, but sometimes on the cheaply produced dolls simply an overwash of color was used.

The Pouties
Pouties with Glass eyes

Beloved by most collectors of character dolls are the pouties. These somber-faced little people seem such a drastic departure from the standard German dolly that it is a wonder people did not run out and buy them right away. Apparently these dolls were such a change from the accepted standard doll look, that they took some getting use to. Yet the time was apparently now right for these dolls which were actually real children captured in miniature form. As with real children, the Heubach children are not always smiling and laughing; sometimes their emotions tend in the other direction: somber, thoughtful, pensive or sad. They have real expressions copied from real children.

Illustrations 8 & 9. One of the favorite Heubach pouties is mold number 6969. This face has such a sweet sensitive look that collectors just want to pick up the doll and take it home. The eyes and the mouth are the outstanding features which make this mold a character doll. The sleep eyes are set into tiny eye sockets surrounded by lightly painted lashes. The mouth with full lips is turned down. The eyebrows are feathered in a natural style. These particular dolls have blue sleep eyes and blonde mohair wigs. They were family dolls, and are entirely original. The lady from whom they were purchased referred to them as a boy and girl; however, the boy is outfitted in a dress when most boys of this period would have worn a romper-type suit. Both of the dolls are 15in (38.1cm) tall and have excellent quality jointed composition bodies stamped with the winged trademark of Cuno and Otto Dressel on the back shoulders, showing that this producer did indeed buy heads from the Heubach Brothers. The girl has her hair styled in braids coiled around her ears which is a typical style for little German girls of the period. She is wearing a blue and white checked cotton dress with lace trim, underclothes, white crocheted stockings and white leather shoes with pom-poms. The boy has short blonde hair and a plaid blue and white dress with simple trim. It has a pleat on each side of the front and loops for a belt which is missing. He has plain white cotton stockings and black high-button shoes. These dolls came with a wardrobe of extra clothes: four white dresses, a pair of matching black velvet and white wool coats, two chemises, three pairs of stockings, three Dutch-style hats for the girl and an extra pair of shoes for each doll. *Jan Foulke Collection.*

LEFT: *Illustration 10.* Here is a tiny 10in (25.4cm) version of the 6969 mold. She has blue glass eyes and an auburn mohair wig. Her jointed composition body is of good quality, and she has been redressed in old fabric. Although this mold is particularly desirable, it is only moderately difficult to find. *Gail Hiatt Collection.*

Illustration 11. In the 11½in (29.2cm) size, this doll with mold number 6970 is dressed like the bigger brother of the girl in Illustration 10. He has blue sleep eyes and a caracul wig. This mold is very similar to the 6969 except that the ears appear to be more prominent and the treatment of the mouth and lower face is different. His lips are much more pronounced and slightly parted as though he just might break into a smile; whereas there seems to be little possibility that the 6969 will smile at all! He is also on a jointed composition body of good quality. This mold seems harder to find than the 6969. *Gail Hiatt Collection.*

Illustration 12. Here is another boy with the 6970 mold number. He is a large 16in (40.6cm) tall, and as is true with most Heubach dolls and figures, the features of the larger sizes are much sharper and have much more detail than can be included in the smaller sizes. Speak of realism in dolls! This boy is so real looking that he could be easily mistaken for a photograph of a boy of 1911. He has blue sleep eyes, a brown mohair wig and clothes which are possibly original. *Mike White Collection.*

Illustration 13. This 12in (30.5cm) girl could probably be taken for a 6969, if you did not look at the number on the back of her head which is 7246. Comparing her to the 6969 shows that while her mouth treatment is very similar, her eyes are larger. She is on a jointed composition body. Her clothes and wig are replacements. *Old Curiosity Shop.*

Illustration 14. This doll has the same mold number as Illustration 13, but looks dissimilar because the artist has given a different treatment to the face. The eyebrows are softer, thinner and at a different angle. The mouth is painted wider and thinner also. The eye sockets have been cut larger. She is 13in (33.0cm) tall on a very nice ball-jointed composition body. Her wig is replaced, but her clothes appear original. *Mackemull Collection.*

Illustration 15. Although this is not a very good photograph, it needs to be included since it is another face in this series, this time mold number 7248. She is very similar to the 7246 doll, except that her eyes are tinier and her lips are thinner. She is 9in (22.9cm) tall, with blue sleep eyes and a blonde mohair wig. She is on a five-piece papier-mâché body of fair quality and has on her original clothes. *Ruby K. Arnold.*

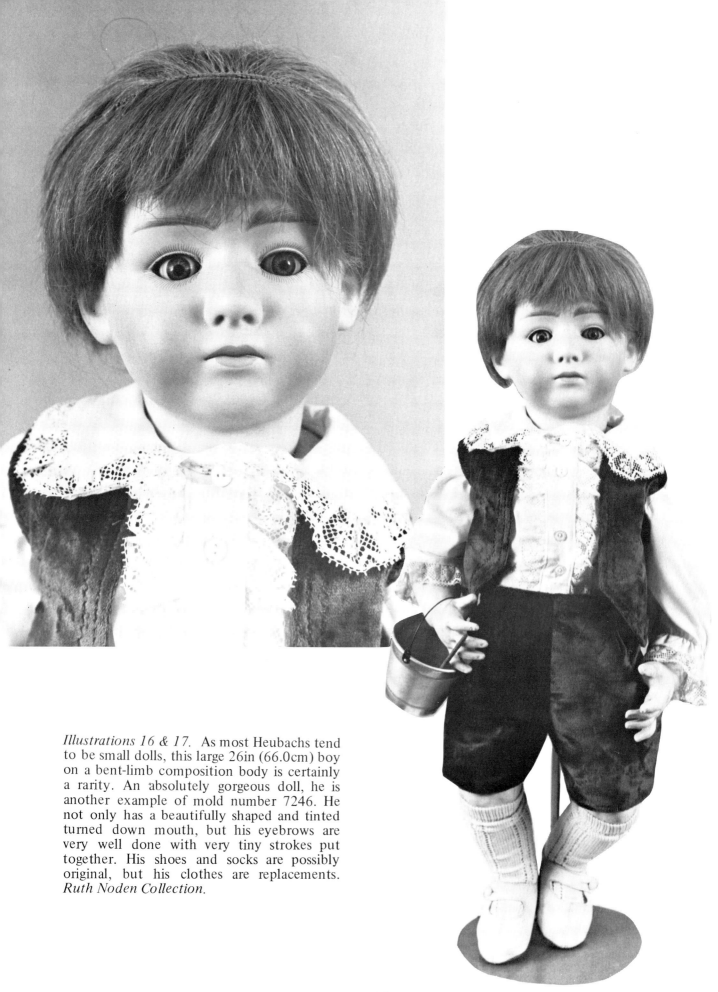

Illustrations 16 & 17. As most Heubachs tend to be small dolls, this large 26in (66.0cm) boy on a bent-limb composition body is certainly a rarity. An absolutely gorgeous doll, he is another example of mold number 7246. He not only has a beautifully shaped and tinted turned down mouth, but his eyebrows are very well done with very tiny strokes put together. His shoes and socks are possibly original, but his clothes are replacements. *Ruth Noden Collection.*

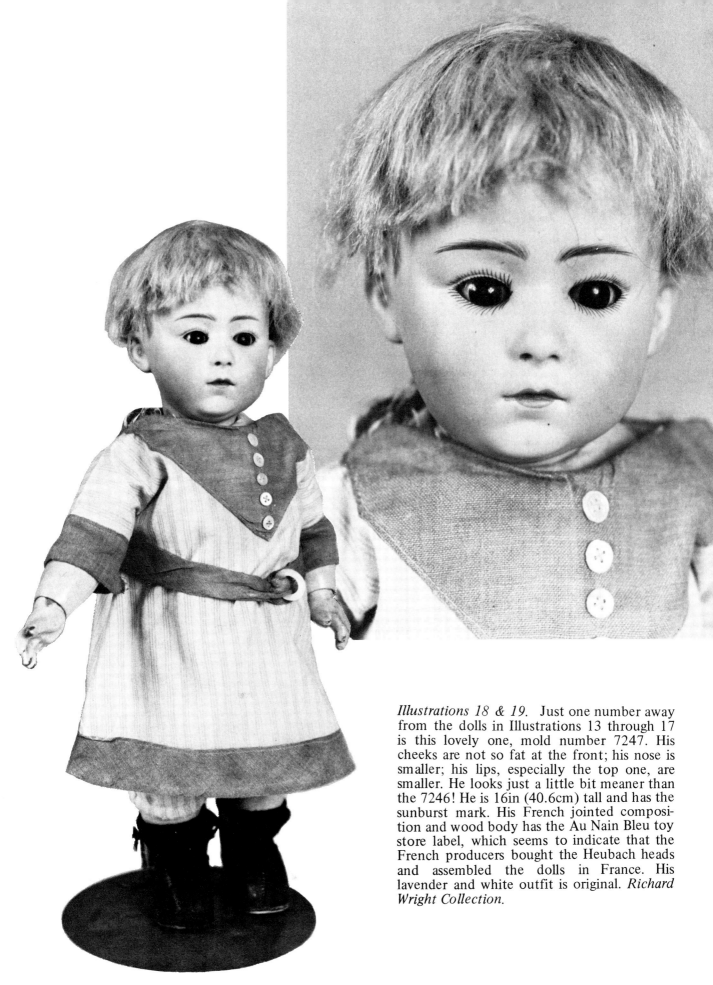

Illustrations 18 & 19. Just one number away from the dolls in Illustrations 13 through 17 is this lovely one, mold number 7247. His cheeks are not so fat at the front; his nose is smaller; his lips, especially the top one, are smaller. He looks just a little bit meaner than the 7246! He is 16in (40.6cm) tall and has the sunburst mark. His French jointed composition and wood body has the Au Nain Bleu toy store label, which seems to indicate that the French producers bought the Heubach heads and assembled the dolls in France. His lavender and white outfit is original. *Richard Wright Collection.*

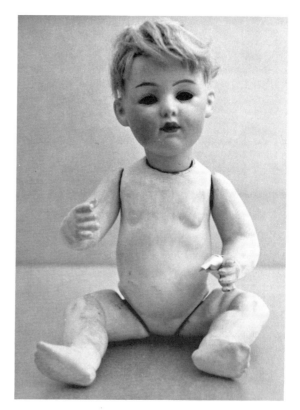

Illustration 20. One of the dearest little babies is this 8in (20.3cm) one with mold number 7256. She has tiny glass eyes, a blonde baby mohair wig and the cutest pouty mouth. Her jointed baby body is of a very poor quality; however, her clothes are all original and quite fancy. Often when companies were presenting beautifully dressed babies, they were careless of the bodies, figuring that they did not show anyway underneath all of the clothes. *Richard Wright Collection.*

Illustration 21. One of the most charming Heubach babies is this 12in (30.5cm) pouty incised 7407 only, no Heubach mark. His eyes are very expressive, but his most outstanding features are his deep cheek dimples and his lips, which are thick and almost puffy, but they are pulled to the front to make his mouth narrow. His wig is original, as is his very nice quality composition bent-limb baby body. *Dorothea and Ronald Baer Collection.*

Illustration 22. The mold number of this girl is recorded as 7497, but her features appear to be identical to the doll in Illustration 21, and as difficult as Heubach numbers are to make out sometimes, the 0 and 9 may have been mistaken. Her quality and decoration are lovely, and she is on a jointed composition body. She is incised with a sunburst. *Old Curiosity Shop.*

Illustration 23. This 9in (22.9cm) doll is marked with a sunburst and 8017. She has lovely coloring and lightly stroked eyebrows. Her sleep eyes are a gray blue color. She appears to be just about like several dolls already shown and illustrates the fact that there is often very little if any difference between Heubach faces which have different mold numbers. And, of course, this does present a problem in trying to classify the work of this company. It makes one wonder if sometimes the same face was given several numbers, maybe to indicate that it was made for several different producers. This doll is on a baby body, but the face is thinner like an older child would have and could also have been used on a jointed composition body. *Ruth Noden Collection.*

Illustration 24. Another doll which is very similar to the face on the doll in Illustration 23, yet a trifle different in the mouth and just a little chubbier in the lower cheeks to represent a younger child, is this toddler marked with mold number 8420. This style body is unusual for a Heubach head, but appears to be original for him. He still has the remains of his original wig. *H&J Foulke.*

Illustration 25. Here is another example of mold number 8420, again showing a different treatment. The eyebrows are simple one-stroke lines instead of being feathered like those of the doll in Illustration 24. The mouth is painted in a different way, particularly the lower lip, which is fully molded, but only partially painted. Her bent-limb baby body is of a medium quality and her wig is original. *Mike White Collection.*

Pouties with Intaglio eyes

Although for some strange reason most collectors prefer dolls with glass eyes, the ones with the lovely molded and painted or intaglio eyes are much more artistic. The intaglio eyes are an important Heubach feature. Kestner, Kammer and Rinehardt, and others simply painted, albeit very artistically, the eye on a molded eyeball, whereas Heubach eyes have a sunken pupil and iris to give the illusion of depth. These are called *intaglio* eyes. When the eyes are painted, the pupil is usually larger than the iris. Each iris is given a raised white dot highlight to indicate a light reflection in the eye, as is natural. Upper and lower lids are molded; a dark line outlines the upper lid. Two red dots usually mark the inside corner of the eye. Occasionally upper and lower eyelashes are painted on.

Illustration 26. This pouty boy is considered by many to be one of the most desirable of the Heubach boy dolls. He certainly looks real enough to take by the hand to the ice cream store. Also, he is one which can be found in the larger sizes. The boy pictured is 21in (53.3cm) tall, with a sunburst and 7622, but often this doll appears with no mold number. He has deeply molded blonde curly hair and is a good example to use for studying the intaglio eyes described above. It seems that no detail was overlooked when he was designed. Even his ears are very intricate with molded natural curves. His lips are puffishly childlike. His cheeks have dimples. The French ball-jointed composition and wood body serves again to show that the French distributors purchased heads from the German makers. *Richard Wright Collection.*

Illustrations 27 & 28. Here is the same boy in a 17in (43.2cm) size, also on a jointed composition body. He is marked only with the sunburst, but is obviously from the same mold as the doll in Illustration 26. Being smaller, his ear is not so detailed as the larger boy's. The profile shows his upturned nose, open/closed mouth and double chin. This model also came as a shoulder head doll. *Old Curiosity Shop.*

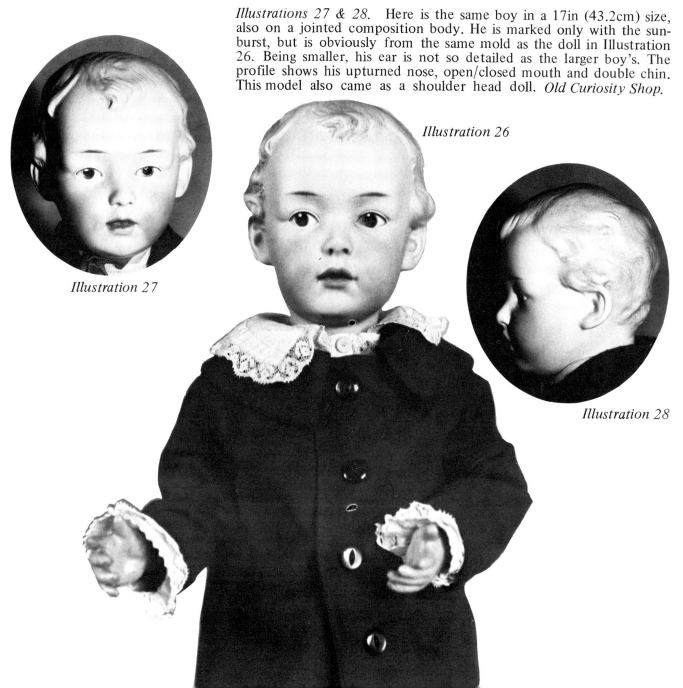

Illustration 26

Illustration 27

Illustration 28

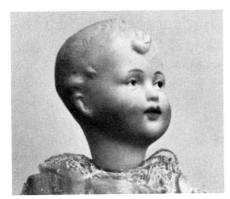

Illustration 29

Illustration 30

Illustration 29. This fellow is just 7½in (19.1cm) tall, but for such a small doll he has a lot of molding detail in his features. His eyes are done the typical Heubach way. The eyebrows are just one brush stroke. The lips are puffy, and he has deep cheek dimples. He is a miniature version of the two larger dolls in Illustrations 26 through 28! Even his hair is molded in exactly the same way. Unfortunately, he has a terrible body, a powdery papier-mâché torso and arms and legs which are not much better. He is, however, wearing his original shift. He is marked with the square mark only. As is the case with many of the small dolls, he does not have a mold number included. Obviously there would have been no place to put it, as this is what he actually has. *H&J Foulke.*

$$\bullet \quad \frac{5}{0} \; \begin{array}{c} D \\ \square \; 12 \end{array}$$

Germany

Illustration 30. Little girls with molded hair, with the exception of the "Coquette" dolls, are much more rare than the little boys. It seems that most of the dolls used as girls had wigs. But here is a sweet, pensive little 10in (25.4cm) girl. She is marked with the square mark and 9167. She has the curly, yet wispy hair of a toddler, and fairly small eyes. Sometimes it is difficult to decide whether these short-haired dolls are boys or girls, but I think she is a girl. She is on a papier-mâché body of not very good quality. *H&J Foulke.*

Illustration 31. This somber-faced fellow is a frequently-found Heubach boy, sometimes as a socket head, but this one is a shoulder head on a very nice cloth body with composition hands. These bodies are generally not as popular with collectors as they are harder to pose and display than the composition ball-jointed bodies. This fellow is marked with the sunburst and 6692. He provides a good link to the next section as this face was also used for the baby dolls. *H&J Foulke.*

The next group of pictures presents the pensive-faced Heubach babies. These are quite easily found and must have been made by the millions! Most of them are in the smaller sizes, and probably only sold for 10 or 15 cents when they were new. These have no mold numbers, simply a square mark, but a baby with this same face has been recorded as mold number 7602.

Illustration 32. Certainly the tiniest Heubach baby we have seen is this little 4½in (11.5cm) one. He just fits in the palm of my hand. It is easy to imagine a little girl's delight in such a doll. On the tiny babies, the heads are bald with hair brush-stroked on. The eyebrows are a simple one-stroke, but the eyes and mouth are nicely done. He is on a five-piece bent-limb baby body. His clothes appear to be original. *Mackemull Collection.*

Illustration 33. This Heubach baby is 6in (15.2cm) and is the same mold as the doll in Illustration 32, but this one has been given the flocked hair, fuzzy to the touch. He is on a five-piece baby body of poor quality, but he does have his original chemise. *Ruby K. Arnold.*

Illustration 35. This 8in (20.3cm) baby is fatter of face than the previous babies. He is on an excellent bent-limb baby body, and was probably a more expensive doll. This head also came on a jointed composition body and could be dressed as a little boy. He has no mold number but a similar baby is recorded as number 9578. *Mackemull Collection.*

Illustration 34. This 6½in (16.5cm) Heubach baby has a very good quality body and is in his original clothes: a pink and white crocheted coat and hat, diaper and tiny leather shoes. He also has an additional coat and hat. This doll is one of a pair of identical twins from the same family who owned the pair of 6969 pouties. *H&J Foulke.*

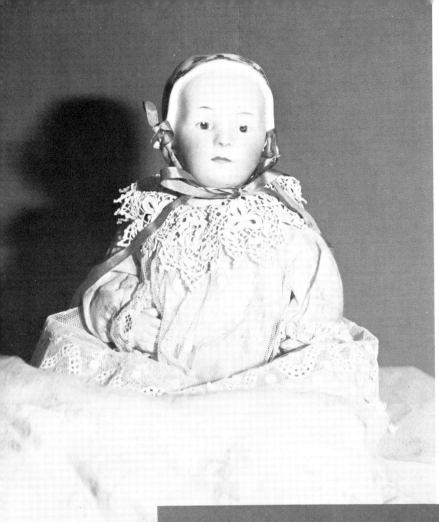

Illustration 36. This lovely 9in (22.9cm) baby, referred to by collectors as the "Stuart Baby," is a very desirable Heubach doll. It is also a link between the figurines with the molded hats and the dolls. It must surely have been the figurines which inspired this concept in doll making, although beginning around 1890 the bisque shoulder head ladies with molded hats were very popular. The molded bonnet of this baby is white with a trim of painted pink flowers and green leaves. Holes are pierced at the sides of the cap for the insertion of ribbon ties. Her face is the standard Heubach pouty baby one. She is marked with a sunburst, but no mold number. *Mackemull Collection.*

Illustration 37. Another 9in (22.9cm) Stuart Baby is positioned so that the flowers on her hat can be more clearly seen. She is also on a bent-limb baby body and is impressed with a sunburst and 7977. *Old Curiosity Shop.*

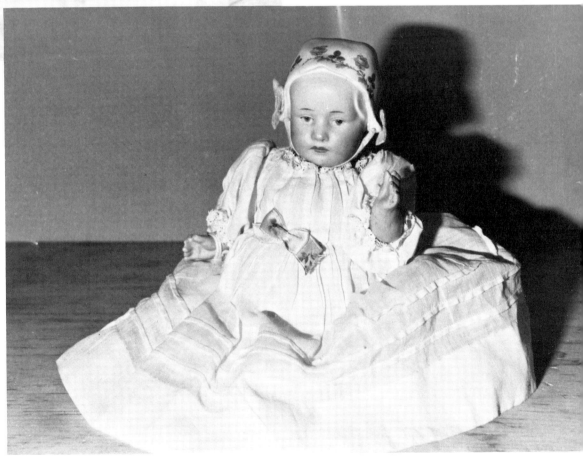

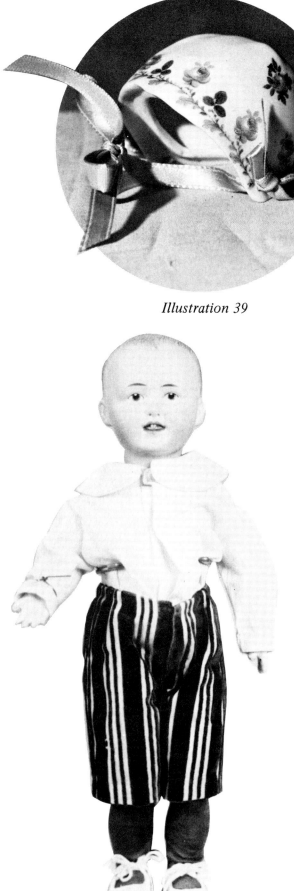

Illustration 39

Illustration 38

Illustration 38. This 14in (35.6cm) Stuart Baby also has the mold number 7977, and is the same as the others except that the flower trim on her hat is different; it is a border of tiny blue flowers with green leaves. *Richard Wright Collection.*

Illustration 39. A rare glass-eyed version of the Stuart Baby has a removable bisque cap like this one to allow for the setting of the glass eyes. Maybe someday the doll which goes with this cap will turn up! *Mackemull Collection.*

Illustration 40. I was not quite sure in which section to place this boy, since he is not smiling, and I am not sure that he is pouting either. But he certainly is being impudent with his tongue sticking out between his lips, and he surely is unusual for a Heubach doll. His head has little evidence of molded hair at all, just brush strokes to indicate that he is not really bald. He has a very high and wide forehead. His eyebrows are just one stroke. His most unusual feature is his mouth with the tongue resting on his lips and the two upper painted teeth. He is 14in (35.6cm) tall on a very good jointed composition body, and is impressed with a square mark and 8878. *Richard Wright Collection.*

Illustration 40

Smiling Children

Many Heubach dolls are just brimming over with the happiness and laughter of life, and a good sampling of these faces is pictured. Of course the term *smiling character* brings to mind primarily the multitude of character babies created by the average German doll company. Cute, yes, but generally of a run-of-the-mill type of smiling face. However, the creations of the Heubach Brothers are distinctively different. Nearly all of them look like some little boy or girl that we once knew or saw.

Illustrations 41 & 42. One of the most sought-after smiling Heubach girls is incised on the back of her head "Dolly Dimple." And, indeed, she is a charming dolly with three very deep dimples. Her lovely eyes radiate happiness; her lips are parted just as though she were ready to burst out telling about her latest adventure. There are very nice details in the decoration of her eyebrows and her lips which are attractively painted with shading on the lower one. Even her ears are quite pronounced. This particular "Dolly Dimple" is 21in (53.3cm) tall, on a very good ball-jointed composition body. She is impressed with the sunburst and 5777 in addition to her name. A very similar character doll is shown in the March 1908 *Playthings* in an ad by Samstag & Hilder Bros. who imported German dolls and toys. The doll in the ad is distinctive for her large eyes, a more open mouth than was usual at the time and shading on the lower lip. If she is a Heubach, this again puts this company early into the manufacture of character dolls. In *Playthings* February 1911, an article on dolls mentions a "Dolly Dimples" [sic] doll, a laughing beauty and further notes that the "youthful radiance of these faces is particularly charming." *Sheila Needle Collection. Photograph by Morton Needle.*

25

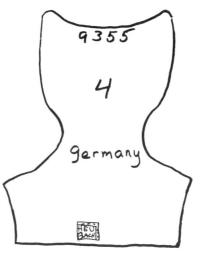

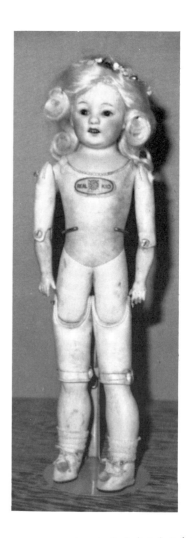

Illustrations 43 & 44. This 18in (45.7cm) girl appears to be another use of the "Dolly Dimple" face, this time as a shoulder head on a real kid body. The molding is the same as the doll in Illustrations 41 and 42, and several features can be noted in this front view which were not so easily seen on the first doll. The nose is rather wide and short, and there is a very distinctive double chin. However, the painting of the mouth is entirely different; the lips are not as full as those on the other doll, and the bottom one lacks the shading detail. This doll is marked with a square and the numbers 9355, but she is not incised "Dolly Dimple" and was perhaps made for a different company. Her present owner found her in an old toy store still tied in her original box. She is wearing her original blonde mohair wig with a bow in her hair and her original shoes and socks. Of course, many dolls were sold unclad to be dressed at home. Her brown sleep eyes are accented with beautiful blonde eyelashes. The line drawings by the owner show her markings and the label on her original box. She appears to be the doll which is advertised on page 4 of the *1914 Marshall Field & Company* catalog, except that her knee joint is different. The doll's wholesale price was $13.50 per dozen. She was listed as a doll with character face, dimpled cheeks, moving eyes and kid body. *Jilda Sallade Collection.*

LEFT: Illustration 45. Obviously a relative of the two girls in Illustrations 41 through 44 is this 20in (50.8cm) doll incised "Santa" and the Heubach sunburst. She is indeed a rarity. A similarity can be seen in the full lips of the mouth, although the "Santa" has no shading on the lower lip, and in the smiling blue sleep eyes and eye lashes. But the dimples are conspicuously absent on "Santa," and the nose is not so wide across the bridge. Her eyebrows are thick and very glossy, a departure from the usual feathery treatment used by the Heubach artists. *Old Curiosity Shop.*

Illustration 46

Illustration 47

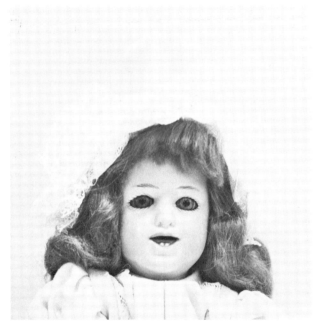

Illustrations 46 & 47. One of the most rare of the Heubach characters with glass eyes is this grinning boy incised with a square mark and 8316. He is 17in (43.2cm) tall on an all-wood jointed body. The fact that one of his eyes has been set in at an off-angle certainly contributes to his mischievous look. Most spectacular, however, is his broad mouth with a row of seven enameled teeth. His dark eyes and hair give good contrast to the lovely flesh coloring of his face. Obviously he is an older child than many of the Heubachs, judging by his features. His nose is sharper, he has no double chin and his lower face is thinner. *Richard Wright Collection.*

Illustration 48. There are probably more Heubach variations of this "laughing child" than any other Heubach mold. Apparently this was a very popular style for them, with the molded, fairly wide open/closed mouth and the two lower molded teeth. This particular little girl has the sunburst mark and mold number 5636. Her large blue eyes give her a very intelligent look. She has a chubby lower face with a double chin. Just 11in (27.9cm) tall, she is on a very good ball-jointed composition body. *Gail Hiatt Collection.*

27

Illustration 49. Here is a little girl with the same happy face, as the doll in Illustration 48, this time in a smaller 8½in (21.6cm) size on a chubby toddler body. She has no mold number but is impressed with the square mark. *Richard Wright Collection.*

ABOVE: Illustration 50. At first glance this boy looks like the same mold as the two girls in Illustrations 48 and 49, but closer inspection shows that his mouth is not nearly so broad and that his bottom lip is lower. This, of course, makes him thinner through the lower face than the girls; his dimples are more pronounced. He is 14in (35.6cm) tall, on an excellent composition jointed body. His clothes are possibly original. Unfortunately, he has no mold number, but he does have the sunburst mark. *Richard Wright Collection.*

Smiling Dolls with Intaglio Eyes

LEFT: Illustration 51. The molding on this 16in (40.6cm) happy, smiling baby has to be recognized for its outstanding attention to detail. This is basically the same face as the preceding doll's, except that this one has deeply incised dark intaglio eyes and molded blonde hair with just enough raised portion to softly frame his face. He is on a five-piece toddler body of good quality and is marked with the round green "Made in Germany" stamp as well as a green stamped 28. *Richard Wright Collection.*

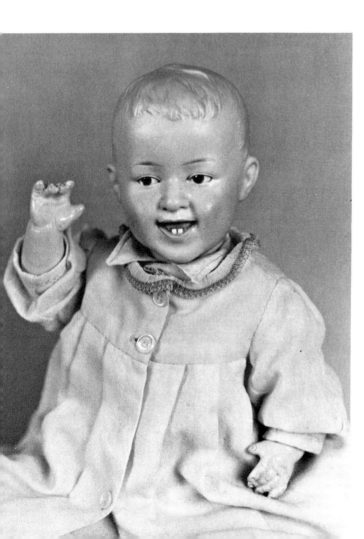

RIGHT: Color Illustration 2.
LEFT: This 21in (53.3cm) pouty boy is incised with a sunburst and 7622. He is described on page 20, Illustrations 26, 27 & 28. RIGHT: One of the most rare of the Heubach characters with glass eyes is this 17in (43.2cm) boy. For further information see page 27, Illustrations 46 & 47. The 9" dog with molded cap and bib is also a Heubach product having the sunburst mark.

LEFT: Color Illustration 1. This 17in (43.2cm) dandy in full day dress is discussed in full detail on page 63, Illustration 140.

Color Illustration 3. FRONT ROW: 4in (10.2cm) action figure is discussed on page 54, Illustration 112. LEFT TO RIGHT: Surprised fellow with side-glancing large round eyes discussed on page 50, Illustration 102. 6in (15.2cm) unmarked doll shown on page 49, Illustration 99. Knock-kneed, pigeon-toed child with large eyes discussed on page 51, Illustration 104. Smug look doll with tiny molded pony tail discussed on page 51, Illustration 103.

Color Illustration 4. Further details about this 14" boy are given on page 28, Illustration 50.

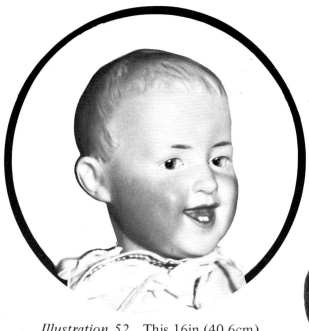

Illustration 54. Another version of these dolls occurs as a shoulder head which can be mounted on a cloth or kid body. Just 10in (25.4cm) tall, this boy is incised only with Germany, but an identical doll has a square mark and the mold number 6736. *Old Curiosity Shop.*

Illustration 52. This 16in (40.6cm) boy is of the same mold as the doll in Illustration 51, but this side view gives a better look at the molding of the ear and hair. It also is an interesting angle from which to look at the intaglio eyes; one can see how depth was achieved, especially in his left eye. He is on a jointed toddler body and marked with a sunburst. A doll of apparently identical mold has been reported with a 6897 number. *Old Curiosity Shop.*

Illustration 53. A member of the same family, but his mouth is not so wide open, is this 9½in (24.2cm) boy with the same two lower teeth! His eyes do not show up as well because they are a light color. However, his deep dimples are very noticeable. He is incised with a sunburst and 7604. *Old Curiosity Shop.*

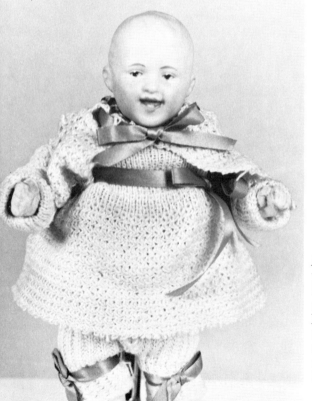

Illustration 55. This 6½in (16.5cm) baby appears to be a much younger version of the previous laughing dolls. Not only does he have less hair and a rounder face, he was also probably a cheaper model, as he does not have the detail of modeling for which Heubach is known. He is on a papier-mâché baby body of inferior quality, but does appear to be wearing his original clothes. These are apparently the dolls which Heubach mass produced for the cheaper market and probably retailed for 10 or 15 cents. *Richard Wright Collection.*

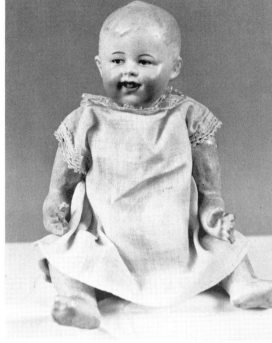

Illustration 57. This small sweet-faced baby is 10½in (26.7cm) long, on a body of papier-mâché which certainly does not match the quality of his head. His mouth is a departure from the preceding dolls since he does not have molded teeth. Instead, he has a little tongue which sticks out between his lips. He is wearing his original chemise and is impressed with a square mark and 7971 or 7911. *Ruth Noden Collection.*

Illustration 56. This fellow has quite a few departures from the previous dolls. The most prominent is his wig. One would just expect him to have molded hair, judging from experiences with Heubach dolls. I have been calling this doll a boy, but perhaps it is a girl, as she does have on a knit blue dress which is perhaps original. I like the prominent ears on this doll, and the fact that the mouth is more closed, instead of so wide open. She has the ubiquitous two molded teeth and the deep cheek dimples. She is 10½in (26.7cm) tall, on a fairly nice composition baby body. High on her crown is her mold number 7307. *Richard Wright Collection.*

Illustration 58. Again, we are getting back to the teeth, but this time the boy has two rows in a fairly wide-open mouth. He has a pleasant look with side-glancing eyes, yet I do not think he qualifies for the googly section which must have some special quality about the face other than simply side-glancing eyes. This boy is 14in (35.6cm) tall and is a shoulder head doll, marked simply with a Heubach square. Another doll of this same mold has the number 8306. *Old Curiosity Shop.*

Illustration 59. This head appears to be a younger version of the one in Illustration 58. This doll does not have as much hair, although it is in the same style. He also has only upper teeth, although these do not show up well in the photo. He is just 9in (22.9cm) tall, on a jointed composition body and is impressed with a square mark and 8191. *Old Curiosity Shop.*

LEFT: Color Illustration 5. This boy and girl pair both bearing the mark 8192 are discussed further on page 46, Illustration 90.

ABOVE: Color Illustration 6. 26in (66.0cm) boy on a bent-limb composition body is described in detail on page 16, Illustration 16.

LEFT: Color Illustration 7. 16in (40.6cm) doll has the sunburst mark and mold number 7247. For more details see Illustrations 18 & 19 on page 17.

Color Illustrations 8 & 9.
Indian pair incised with square
mark and 8457. For more details
see Illustration 2, page 5.

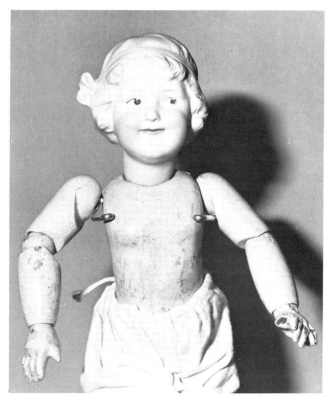

Illustration 60. The best known of the Heubach girls, perhaps because she is the most easily recognizable is the "Coquette," which is found in fair abundance. Her blonde hair has masses of lovely short curls in the latest fashion of the day, and her head is surrounded by a ribbon which is usually painted turquoise. She has an unmistakably flirtatious look with her lips pressed together in mirth as though she is trying to stifle a giggle at an inappropriate time. Her side-glancing eyes only contribute to her coquettish look. This particular doll is shown on her French ball-jointed composition and wood body. Enough Heubachs have been found on French bodies to substantiate the theory that French producers bought the German heads for their dolls. She is impressed with a square mark and 7788. *Old Curiosity Shop.*

BELOW: Illustration 61. Here is a 12in (30.5cm) "Coquette" shown from a different angle. She is on a German jointed composition body and is wearing clothes which are possibly original. She is also incised with a square mark and 7788. Judging from the numbers of these dolls available, it must have been a very popular model. *Old Curiosity Shop.*

Illustration 62. This beautiful example of a "Coquette" head is on a flapper-type body with slim arms and legs. This is an unusual body for the "Coquette," but much more appropriate to her than the chunky bodies, especially the French one. The slim body makes her look quite a bit more grown-up. She appears to be wearing her original clothes and shoes. This view gives emphasis to her dimples and her side-glancing eyes. This doll also has a row of painted teeth which the other two "Coquettes" lack. Her head is marked with a sunburst and 7763. Another "Coquette" has been reported with a mold number of 7768, and at this point we are not sure whether there were three different mold numbers or whether the numbers might have been recorded incorrectly as sometimes they are very difficult to read. This doll also comes as a shoulder head which is shown in the introductory section. *Mackemull Collection.*

"Bonnie Babe"

Nearly everyone is familiar with "Bonnie Babe" created by Georgene Averill in 1926. The famous Averill baby, almost ugly in its reality, is a popular collector's item. Attached to a cloth body with composition arms and legs, the solid dome head has wisps of molded hair. The forehead is broad and high; the ears stick out; the open mouth is fairly large with a tongue and two teeth. "Bonnie Babe" has dimples on her chubby cheeks and, of course, two chins. The "Bonnie Babe" made all of bisque is a darling toddler doll, with swivel neck and joints at hips and shoulders. Her hair is deeply molded, and she has tiny glass eyes which open and close. Of course, she also has the unmistakable dimples and chubby cheeks, as well as an open mouth with two lower teeth. However, there is another version of "Bonnie Babe" which is very rarely found, and unless you have a sharp eye for faces, you might entirely overlook her as a "Bonnie Babe." This is the rare wigged version which was produced as a socket head on a chubby composition body with molded shoes and socks, the same type of body which is used for the googly dolls. This "Bonnie Babe" has the same little face that is on the all-bisque doll, just as cute and darling! The first of these dolls I acquired is dressed like a little girl. She is 7in (17.8cm) tall with a blonde mohair wig and brown sleep eyes. She is marked with the mold number 1393 high at the crown, and at first I thought she was a Heubach, but now I feel that she is probably not a Heubach because of the low number sequence, and because the numbers are not impressed like Heubach numbers and the Germany is written in a different manner. Possibly she is by Alt, Beck, and Gottschalk who made some of the larger "Bonnie Babe" dolls. However, the second one of these wigged little ones was a treasure just for this book, because he is clearly incised with the Heubach square mark. Also up high on his crown opening are the numbers 12386. His coloring and decoration are different from that of the little girl, suggesting a different manufacturer as well as a different decorator, but the mold is identical. The bodies are identical, suggesting that perhaps the distributor, in this case, George Borgfeldt, ordered heads from two different manufacturers.

LEFT: *Illustration 63.* This is a 7in (17.8cm) wigged "Bonnie Babe" incised 1393. Her bisque is quite pale with very rosy cheeks; her eyebrows are very pale with a smudged look. Her eyelashes are very lightly applied. She has the typical "Bonnie Babe" mouth, although she is lacking her teeth. She also has dimples and a cute pug nose. Her lip color is muted. She has a papier-mâché toddler body with painted shoes and socks. *Jan Foulke Collection.*

RIGHT: *Illustration 64.* Here is an 8in (20.3cm) wigged "Bonnie Babe" impressed with the Heubach square mark and numbers 12386. He has a pinker overall complexion and rosy cheeks. His eyebrows are very light, but painted in one definitive stroke. His eyelashes are heavily applied in the Heubach manner while the lip color is bright. He has the "Bonnie Babe" mouth with two tiny lower teeth. His dimples are there, but are not so pronounced as hers. *Jan Foulke Collection.*

12386

3
—
0

□
Germany

Mechanical Dolls

Dolls that do things are not at all modern inventions. Dolls have been doing things for over a hundred years. There is always a certain fascination about seeing a doll in motion or making some sort of noise, and apparently these types of dolls have always been popular novelty items. Of course, Heubach probably made only the heads for these dolls, the bodies made and the doll assembled by another company or distributor.

Illustrations 65A, 65B & 65C. Again, here is a problem in classifying Heubach heads. One would expect this doll to be of the same mold number as the one in Illustration 68, but not so. He is incised with a sunburst and 7604. A nice large 12in (30.5cm) size, large at least for these mechanical Heubachs, he has the same smiling face with intaglio eyes, pronounced dimples in his cheeks and very nice molding of mouth, lips and teeth. His socket head fits into the mechanical body. When he is wound, he walks first on one leg, then on the other; as he toddles from side to side, he also swivels from the waist. He does look a little ridiculous, but fun nonetheless. *Gail Hiatt Collection.*

Illustration 66. This 12in (30.5cm) Heubach girl is incised only with the sunburst, but her face can be identified as being used on other mechanical dolls as well. Her tiny glass eyes are squinting in a laugh which is apparent on her open/closed mouth. She has a socket head on a mechanical body. Unfortunately all of what is going on cannot be seen in the photograph, as she is trying to ward off a dog by keeping the chair between the two of them. I am not sure she should be smiling; perhaps she should look frightened! *Old Curiosity Shop.*

Illustration 67. This "Pat-a-Cake, Pat-a-Cake Baby" is all original and in working order. He still has his cap with a printed band that identifies him. His action is simple, but cute. When his stomach is pressed, he pats his hands together. This was a type of action often found on old toys, especially clowns with cymbals in their hands. This doll has a stock Heubach shoulder head of the so-called laughing boy with molded hair, intaglio eyes and an open mouth with two lower molded teeth. It must have been a fairly popular head as it is found quite often. This 8in (20.3cm) baby is incised with a square mark and 6736. It is easy to see why such a laughing happy face would be attractive to buyers. Also, it was probably a fairly inexpensive face as it did not have inset eyes or teeth, needed no wig and was a shoulder head which was easier to mount than a socket head. *Mackemull Collection.*

Illustration 68. This little doll has a mechanism in its cardboard cone. When she is wound, she goes forward; at the same time she moves from side to side at the waist and waves her hands up and down. She is in her original clothes and altogether presents a most interesting concept of a baby, but one which would be fairly limited as far as child's play is concerned. Her socket head is incised with a square mark and 7314. She is almost like the "Pat-a-Cake Baby," but on close inspection, her mouth looks a little different in shape. She was available at the wholesale price of $9.00 per dozen in the *1914 Marshall Field & Company* catalog. *Ruth Noden Collection.*

Illustration 70. "Whistling Jim" has his original tag still on him, so we know just who he is. His lips are pursed with a hole through them. When the bellows in his chest is pressed, one hears a very realistic whistle from him! Jim has a flange neck on a pink cloth body with composition arms. He is impressed with a square mark and 8774. His coloring is very natural with nice rosy cheeks. His eyes are deeply incised with painted blue and white dot highlights. His eyebrows are put on in one stroke; his hair is dark blonde, a typical Heubach light coloring. He is wearing completely original clothing, a blue romper suit, lacy socks and imitation leather shoes. A penciled note on the back of his tag dates him for us: "Christmas 1915, From Clara." He was still being offered, or perhaps offered again would be better, since the war caused a cessation of the doll business, in the 1924 Montgomery Ward catalog. By that time he was called "Tom." The ad reads: "Can you whistle? Tom can. Just press his chest and hear him give a fine, loud, boyish whistle. Tom is a good little chap with which to amuse baby." His cost was 89 cents plus 6 cents postage! *Jan Foulke Collection.*

Illustration 69. The face of the 12in (30.5cm) boy matches that of the girl in Illustration 66. His eyelashes are more pronounced and emphasize his tiny glass eyes. Both of the dolls have beautifully painted eyebrows, done in tiny little strokes. The boy, when wound, walks along pulling his cart. *Old Curiosity Shop.*

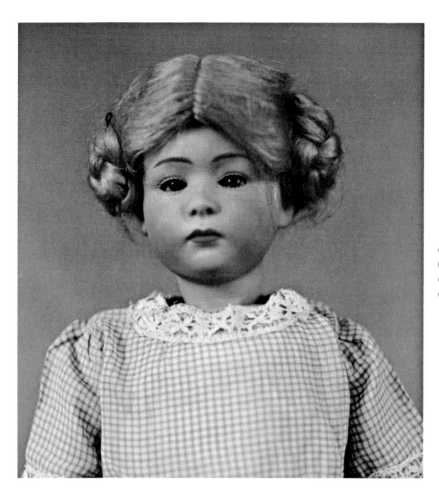

Color Illustration 10. 15in (38.1cm) pouty has a companion doll shown in Illustrations 8 & 9 on page 13.

Color Illustration 11. 22in (55.9cm) boy impressed with mold number 10532. For more details see Illustration 5, page 6.

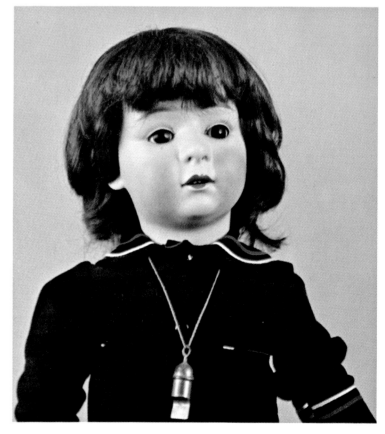

Googlies

The imps of the doll world, the googlies are very popular with collectors and have a wide-ranging appeal. Their prices are high because of their scarcity, as they are a later doll and, therefore, were made for a much shorter period of time as their production was interrupted by World War I in Europe.

Illustrations 72 & 73. This googly girl has beautiful eyebrows, feathered with a myriad of tiny brushstrokes which appear on some of the Heubach dolls. They certainly show that great care was taken in her decoration as opposed to drawing just one line above each eye. Her eye sockets are large, but not as perfectly round as on the "Einco" googly, and her eyes are set to look to the side in a roguish manner. She has pronounced dimples on her chubby cheeks, and her lips are thin as though she is trying to suppress her smile. She is 13in (33.0cm) tall on a composition body and is incised with the square mark. Unfortunately, we were not able to obtain her mold number, if indeed she had one, as many of the Heubachs simply do not. Also, as Heubach mold numbers are done in very small letters up high on the back of the head at the crown opening, it is often difficult to determine just exactly what the numbers are, even with a magnifying glass, if they smear or do not print plainly. Sometimes, of course, they are covered with glue from the wig which makes the numbers impossible to read. *Richard Wright Collection.*

Illustration 71. The most captivating of the Heubach googlies is this 14in (35.6cm) doll which can be made up as a boy or a girl. The eye sockets are perfectly round, and the eyes themselves can be moved to look in different directions by means of a wire lever. This is certainly one of the rarest of all googlies, by Heubach or any other maker. The impertinent face is achieved not only by the prominent eyes, but also by the mouth with a large bottom lip but a tiny upper lip, almost as though she were biting her top lip to keep her mouth closed. Of course, the chubbiness of the face and the little double chin add to her appeal. Her heavy eyebrows are quite high on her forehead and are long for the size of her face, but they are covered by her bangs in the photograph. She also has an impudent nose. All of her facial characteristics put together contribute to make her an amusing character. She has a five-piece toddler body of composition. Her head is incised with a square mark and "Einco," the trademark of Eisenmann & Co. for whom Heubach made this doll. It would date around 1911 to 1913. According to Carol Ann Stanton, it was part of the "Kiddieland" series. This doll has also been found as a shoulder head incised with mold number 8164 on a cloth body. *Richard Wright Collection.*

Illustration 74. Certainly a unique doll is this "winker," as I do not know of any other company which made one like this! This little doll has short molded hair and is more often made up as a roguish boy, although this little girl appears to have her original clothes, a gauze dress with red felt hat and coat. She has one blue glass eye and one eye closed, a raised eyebrow on the open eye and a down-slanting eyebrow on the closed eye. Her mouth is also raised on the left side. She is incised only with Germany done in the Heubach manner and is 8in (20.3cm) tall. *Mackemull Collection.*

Illustration 75. This illustration is from our files and goes back a long way so we were unable to obtain the information about the marks, but decided to show him anyway in contrast to the "winker" with the glass eye as this one has a painted eye, with very heavy eyelashes. The other eye is not really all the way closed, either. It is open just a wee amount to allow one to see just a tiny bit of the eyeball, mostly the white part, but just a speck of color in the far corner. He is 9½in (24.2cm) tall. Interestingly enough, a photograph of a Heubach doll on page 295 of the Colemans' *Collector's Encyclopedia of Dolls* appears to be of the same mold but with both eyes painted open, looking sideways and up. Other "winkers" have been reported with mold number 9141. *Richard Wright Collection.*

Illustration 77. A sister to the doll in Illustration 76, this one has the same mold number, but the artist treatment is a little different. The eyebrows are straight, yet feathered on the inside; the lower lip is not so wide. Also in this photograph the ears are prominently displayed, and they really stick out! Even the angle of her eyes is different. The whole doll goes to show how two faces from the same mold can be made to look different from each other. She is 9in (22.9cm) tall also, and on a papier-mâché googly body with painted shoes and socks. Her clothes appear original. *Old Curiosity Shop.*

Illustration 76. This little Heubach googly appears more often than the others, but it does not diminish either her desirability or her appeal. Her little pug nose and her watermelon mouth as well as her side-glancing eyes contribute to her impish expression. (The watermelon mouth gets its name from its resemblance to a slice from a half a watermelon!) Her wig is typical of the bobbed style of mohair or sometimes human hair which was usually found on the googlies. She is dressed in what appears to be her original costume, reminiscent of a storybook character. Her five-piece body is of a better quality than is usually found on these dolls. She is incised with a square mark and 9573. (Again, there was a problem with reading the numbers and I had recorded 0573, which really does not seem a right Heubach sequence and the doll in Illustration 77 came along as 9573.) *Mackemull Collection.*

Illustration 78. This little 7in (17.8cm) googly's name is "Elisabeth" stamped right on the back of her neck in green just above the Heubach square mark. She has darling fat cheeks which take up more than half of her face. Her mouth is just a tiny thing. Her brown sleep eyes look to the side, and she has fairly heavy painted lashes. She is on a typical five-piece papier-mâché body and is wearing her original dress and hat of orange cotton. *Richard Wright Collection.*

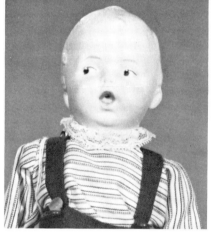

Illustration 81. This googly boy looks as though he is all ready to sing in the choir. His hair is close-molded with just a few curls; tiny intaglio eyes with white highlights look to the side. He is just 7½in (19.1cm) tall on a papier-mâché body with a terrible cardboard torso. He is incised with a square mark and 8729. *H&J Foulke.*

Illustration 79. The head of this boy is reminiscent of those on the all-bisque characters. He has an almost bald head with just a hint of molded curls at the forehead and above his ears. His brown eyes are large, painted to the side, with quite heavy upper lashes; his eyebrows are just lines; his mouth is closed. The most outstanding feature about him is his body, which is made of unusually good composition jointed at the shoulders, elbows, hips and knees with lovely molded and painted one-strap shoes and socks. He is 9in (22.9cm) tall and is incised with a square mark and 8589. *Richard Wright Collection.*

Illustration 80. This is the same mold as the boy in Illustration 79. However, the painting treatment is different. The eyebrows are heavier, the eyes are just a little larger, the eyelashes are heavier and the lips are broader. He is 7in (17.8cm) tall on a chubby googly-type composition body. He is incised with a square mark and 8589. *H&J Foulke.*

Illustraton 82. Perhaps this girl is joining the little boy in Illustration 81 in the choir; if so, she looks a little surprised to know that she can sing! Then again maybe she is just looking at a doll in a store window! She is on a five-piece composition body instead of the usual fatter papier-mâché one on which most of these googlies are found. Just 8in (20.3cm) tall, she is incised with a square mark and 9081. She appears to be wearing her original clothes. *Richard Wright Collection.*

Traditional Styles

The output of the Gebruder Heubach factory included very few of the "dolly-faced" girls or ordinary character dolls. These types of dolls were the staple products of most of the other German doll factories. Even after the coming of the character doll, though the dolly dolls remained very popular, the brothers Heubach made very few models of this type of doll. One of which we do not have a photograph to include is a shoulder head girl doll with an open mouth, sleep eyes and wig. Impressed with the mold number 10633 and the Heubach square mark, she is like millions of her sisters turned out by the run-of-the-mill German factories. This one was marketed by Sears, Roebuck & Co. as one of their "Dainty Dorothy" dolls. It is almost a shock to see the Heubach mark on her!

ABOVE: Illustration 83. One of the more ordinary-looking dolls made by Heubach is this little child incised with a square mark on the neck and numbers which look like 7711. (Again Heubach used tiny numbers high on the crown opening of these dolls that wore wigs, and often they are only lightly impressed or blurred.) She has sleep eyes and an open mouth with four upper teeth. As with other Heubachs, her ears are not pierced. Her eyebrows are nicely feathered in the Heubach manner, and her eyelashes are also well done. She is on a rather ordinary jointed composition body. Her wig needs a little attention, but appears to have been styled in a bob. *Old Curiosity Shop.*

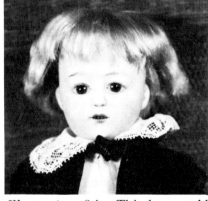

Illustration 84. This boy mold number 10532 is just 8½in (21.6cm) tall on a fairly standard papier-mâché body of five parts. *H&J Foulke.*

Another open-mouth Heubach is this attractive mold number 10532. This doll has been recorded in sizes from 8in (20.3cm) to 22in (55.9cm), the latter being a fairly large size for a Heubach as most tend to be smaller. Judging from the numbers seen, it was a popular model as it does turn up quite often. The doll does not have the vacant look of many open-mouth German dolls, and, in fact, has quite a sweet face. Four examples of this model are shown in Illustrations 84 through 87. All dolls of this mold usually have sleep eyes, feathered eyebrows and four upper teeth. All are incised with the square mark on the neck and 10532 at the crown opening.

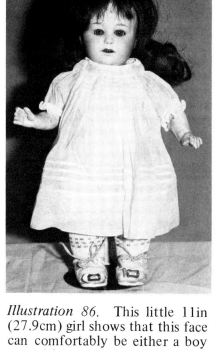

Illustration 85. This fellow is 11½in (29.2cm) tall on a good quality jointed composition body. *Mary Goolsby Collection.*

Illustration 86. This little 11in (27.9cm) girl shows that this face can comfortably be either a boy or a girl according to the owner's preference. Her wig is new, and the clothes, while old, are not original to her. She is on a chunky five-piece toddler body of medium quality. *Mackemull Collection.*

Illustration 87. The beautiful complexion of this doll can be seen in the color section on page 40. His eyes are brown and his mohair wig is auburn. In this illustration it looks as though his mouth is closed, but it is not; the lips are slightly parted, but the teeth are set back fairly far and do not show here. He is 22in (55.9cm) tall on a very good quality composition toddler body. *Ruth Noden Collection.*

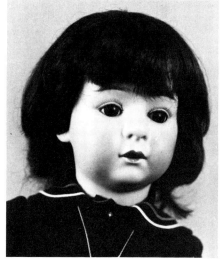

RIGHT: Illustration 88. This 23in (58.4cm) baby is not only an unusually large size for a Heubach, it has an unusual mark. Along with the incised square mark and the number 10586 are inscribed a large W u Z over I, indicating that the doll was made for another company, perhaps Wagner & Zetzsche of Ilmenau, Thuringia. Again the face is sweet, but not outstanding as far as character dolls go. She has blue sleep eyes, an open mouth with four upper teeth, nice fat cheeks and pretty eyebrows. Her clothes and hair are old. She is on a bent-limb baby body of excellent quality. *Ruth Noden Collection.*

10586

W u Z

y.

Germany

□

Another open-mouth Heubach which turns up fairly regularly but still seems to maintain a good price is mold number 8192, which seems to be a favorite of many collectors of cute dolls. These dolls nearly always have excellent quality heads with rosy complexions. They have large soulful eyes which sleep, chubby cheeks and open mouths with four upper teeth. The eyebrows and eyelashes are always well painted. The odd thing is that they are found on a variety of bodies of different quality, perhaps indicating that this was a standard head which Heubach sold to other companies which produced the complete doll. Heads with this mold number have also been found on excellent quality five-piece composition bodies with painted shoes and socks, up to about a 12in (30.5cm) size, as well as on the slim composition bodies with the high knee joints, indicating these dolls were made until about 1930.

Illustration 89. A beautiful number 8192 head done up as a girl with replaced wig and clothes. *H&J Foulke.*

Illustration 90. This boy and girl pair of dolls are both marked 8192. They are on very nice good quality jointed composition bodies. The boy has a replaced wig and clothes. The girl has a replaced wig and hat, but may have original clothes. This pair can also be seen in the color section on page 32. *Rosemary Dent Collection.*

Christmas Novelties

For the doll makers, Christmas was the big season. They prepared over a year ahead, as companies placed their Christmas orders during the first three or four months of each year. And, of course, the wider range of goods at varying prices which a company could offer, the greater would be their sales potential. The Christmas novelties are often in the form of candy box containers, some of the smaller ones possibly meant to be hung on the Christmas tree. Some of the tiny children were often used in Christmas scenes under the tree.

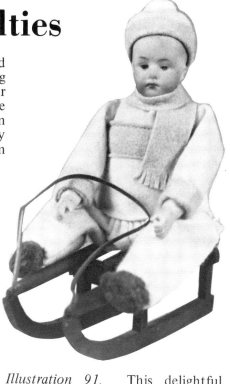

LEFT: *Illustration 92.* Here is another tiny Heubach boy made up with a candy box inside his torso. His head, lower arms and legs are bisque. He is wearing his original fleece or felt snow suit, cap and muffler. Including the sled, he is just 6in (15.2cm) tall. *Ruth Noden Collection.*

Illustration 91. This delightful pouty boy riding his wooden sled is actually a candy box. A round cylinder forms his torso which lifts off to reveal a compartment to fill with candies. He is wearing his original fleece outdoor clothes. Just 7½in (19.1cm) tall including the sled, he is impressed with the sunburst mark. *Mackemull Collection.*

Illustration 93. This 8in (20.3cm) tall pouty-faced boy is also a candy box, coming apart so that the torso holds the candies. He is wearing his original white plush suit with blue trim. His hands are bisque. *Mackemull Collection.*

Many collectors feel that these tiny bisque faces used to make up children as decorations on Christmas candy containers or as ornaments to hand on the Christmas tree were also made by Heubach. Although they are unmarked, many Heubach characteristics are apparent in these little faces. The little bodies of these dolls are made of wire covered with layers of crepe paper or cotton batting or a combination of both. The clothes actually form the covering of the wire.

ABOVE: Illustration 94. This sweet-faced googly-eyed girl sitting on a square candy container is just 4in (10.2cm) tall. She is dressed in blue and white cotton batting and holds a bunch of red berries. *Mackemull Collection.*

UPPER RIGHT: Illustration 95. It is doubtful that this little girl is really as mean as she looks, but possibly someone is trying to push her off the log as she is really getting close to the edge. The log forms a candy container. She is dressed in blue cotton batting and is 5½in (14.0cm) tall. *Mackemull Collection.*

Illustration 96. The child riding the front of this sled is an all-bisque nodder, probably not a Heubach. The child in the rear is of the type attributed to Heubach. He is wearing his original snow suit of cotton batting. *Mackemull Collection.*

LEFT: Illustration 97. Just 4in (10.2cm) tall including the base is this candy box with a little girl ornament. Judging by the expression on her face, she is taking herself quite seriously. She is dressed in a red and blue Christmas outfit which is original. *Mackemull Collection.*

All-Bisque Characters

Molded Shoes

Tiny dolls have always been popular with little girls. There is something special and cozy about a doll which is just small enough to fit comfortably in one tiny hand. These are the treasured dolls of childhood, and today many are found which have been packed away in small boxes, often with complete wardrobes of handmade clothes, many times the loving labor of a small girl just learning to use a needle. These small dolls illustrate again the infinite number of faces of varying expressions which appeared on the dolls of the Brothers Heubach, surpassing those by any other doll producer, ever. These small dolls must have been a popular product and a good selling one also, or it would not have been profitable for the company to produce so many different dolls since mold making was one of the most costly items in doll production.

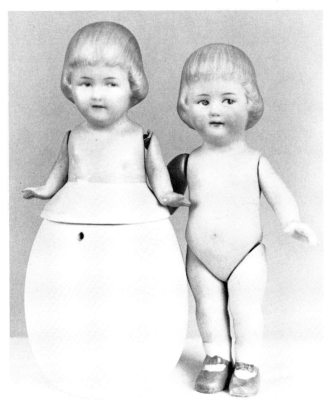

Illustration 99. The doll on the right has the same limbs as her larger sister in Illustration 98. Her fingers are delicate and her molded shoes are identical, but her socks are not so finely ribbed. This doll has also been found with stationary pedestal legs. Her bobbed hairdo is not fancy, but nicely and and cleanly styled. Her hair color is sandy with darker brush marks to provide shading. These two items make an interesting pair because, while the molding is the same, the decoration of the facial features of the doll is done with much more care than those of the girl on the egg box. The doll's eyes are larger and heavier, giving her a more alert look. Her mouth is better defined and has a shading line. The doll is 6in (15.2cm) tall and unmarked; the egg is impressed with the Heubach square mark and stands 6½in (16.5cm) tall. The *1914 Marshall Field & Company* catalog shows this doll in an 8in (20.3cm) size at the wholesale price of $6.00 per dozen. *Richard Wright Collection.*

Illustration 98. This 9in (22.9cm) girl is certainly a very desirable size in an all-bisque doll, as the majority found are much smaller. Her brown hair is lovely with brushmarks on her forehead and well-defined curls at the sides and around the back of her head. Her three hair bows are lavender and a molded ribbon runs around the back of her head to connect the two side bows. Her head is slightly turned; her brown eyes are looking to the side; and her lips are parted showing two tiny teeth. She looks like she is just getting ready to give a flirtatious response to a question. Her hands have the typical Heubach shape with the second and third fingers molded together. Her footwear is also seen on many Heubach all-bisque girls. The brown shoes have bows molded on the straps and her low white socks are vertically ribbed. She is incised 10490 over 3 between her shoulders. *Ruth Noden Collection.*

Illustration 100. This little doll is a surprising 8in (20.3cm) tall! She seems smaller because she has almost a baby look, and although she appears shy, her clenched fists indicate she is getting ready either to swing them or pound them! Her stationary pedestal legs and shoes are typical Heubach features except that her shoes are blue and the straps are narrower. Her white socks are not ribbed. A departure from the norm, her hands have clenched fists, a feature appearing on at least one other Heubach figure illustrated, and appear to be original to the doll. Her short blonde hair, wispy on the forehead with tiny side curls, indicates a much younger child than the previous dolls. Her pink cotton dress appears to be contemporary with the doll. Her eyebrow painting is interesting, as is her tiny open/closed mouth. She is incised with a square mark and 13. *Richard Wright Collection.*

Illustration 101. This little 4in (10.2cm) girl has blue slippers with pointed toes just like those of the "Chin Chin Babies." Her mouth is marvelously done in a pouty triangle shape. Her large side-glancing eyes have a lovely white highlight, as well as heavily painted upper eyelashes. She has a glossy blue bow above each ear. A boy doll with a watermelon mouth was made as a companion to her. She is incised with the Heubach square mark. *H&J Foulke.*

Bare Feet

Although the following three dolls are not marked, they appear to be of Heubach manufacture when the general style, construction and finishing is compared to known Heubach dolls. This is especially evident in the treatment of the large eyes with heavy upper lashes, the chubby torsos, the expressive mouths and the nearly bald heads. They were perhaps part of a series as they have many characteristics in common. They are 5in (12.7cm) tall. Their arms are alike with fingers molded together instead of separated as on the previous dolls which at first suggested replaced arms on the first that I examined. However, the next two are exactly the same which perhaps suggests cheaper production methods and perhaps later dolls. They have bare feet instead of the usual molded shoes and socks.

Illustration 102. This surprised fellow has large round side-glancing eyes, with an interesting white highlight, another Heubach characteristic. He has fairly heavy upper lashes like the previous little girl. His head is nearly bald, but he does have a few strands of hair stroked on in a sparse fashion. *Richard Wright Collection.*

RIGHT: Illustration 103. This sister is especially interesting, not only because of the smug look on her face, but for two other reasons. Although she appears to be bald, actually her hair is pulled to the back, and she has a tiny molded pony tail on the back of her head. In addition, she is one of the few all-bisques wearing her original clothes, including darling tiny black leather shoes. Her round eyes also have heavily painted upper lashes and white dot highlights. Her turned down mouth makes her especially appealing. *Richard Wright Collection.*

LEFT: Illustration 104. Also in her original clothes, a gauze chemise and cap as well as the same leather shoes as the girl in Illustration 103, is this knock-kneed, pigeon-toed child with marvelously large eyes. Her triangular shaped mouth is unusual in most dolls, but not in Heubachs. Her uplifted eyebrows add to her surprised look. *Richard Wright Collection.*

Chin Chin Babies

These appealing little Oriental characters range around 4½in (11.5cm) in height, give or take a little. Their smooth excellent quality bisque is golden yellow. The general design shows the influence of the ubiquitous Kewpie dolls by Rose O'Neill. They have chunky torsos, short fat pedestal legs and jointed shoulders with arms gracefully sloping outward. The fingers are quite distinctive, pointed, with the second and third molded together as shown in the illustration, so it is easy to tell whether or not the dolls have proper arms. Their faces are done in several styles. The molded caps vary, with at least six styles on record, including one with a molded orange cap not shown here. The boys have shiny black molded queues. The feet have molded slippers with pointed toes. The dolls are usually, but not always, stamped on the feet with a Heubach square mark. Originally the dolls wore a triangular paper label (yellow, red and black on white) on their front torsos. One little "Chin Chin Baby" that I owned had a fan-shaped label tied to her wrist.

The collector wishing to gather Heubach "Chin Chin Babies" should be careful to differentiate them from the very similar "Queue San Babies" made in Japan for Morimora Brothers. It is easy to confuse these with the "Chin Chins" because they have the same faces, hands and pointed toes, but the label of the Japanese dolls is diamond-shaped and the bisque and finishing are not so fine. However, the "Queue San Babies" while interesting in their own right, cost less than half the price of the "Chin Chins" on today's collectors' market.

Illustration 105. These two "Chin Chin Babies" have different facial expressions. The boy on the left has his head tilted to one side. The modeling detail around his eyes is very nice for such a small doll. His faintly smiling face seems to be hiding a secret! His cap is yellow with painted black trim; his shoes match his yellow cap. The doll on the right has a lavender cap with red and green trim. This headdress sometimes occurs in other color combinations. His shoes are red and his solemn face has a pouty look. Alas, he has lost his arms and is waiting patiently for a proper pair. *Mackemull Collection.*

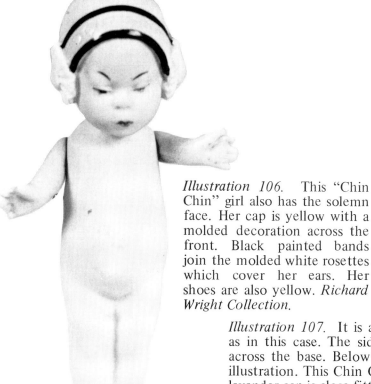

Illustration 106. This "Chin Chin" girl also has the solemn face. Her cap is yellow with a molded decoration across the front. Black painted bands join the molded white rosettes which cover her ears. Her shoes are also yellow. *Richard Wright Collection.*

Illustration 107. It is always great to have a doll with its original label as in this case. The sides of the triangle are lettered CHIN with Baby across the base. Below Baby is Germany which does not show in the illustration. This Chin Chin also has the more common pouty face. The lavender cap is close fitting with shiny pink trim around the face and on the ribs. The shoes are pink also. *H&J Foulke.*

Position Babies

Position babies appear to be a staple item in the Butler Brothers wholesale catalog of 1899. Although the ones pictured are probably not Heubachs, they do show the apparent popularity of these little figures, either nude or in molded shifts posed in "assorted positions as natural as life." Four sets were offered: Filipino, much like the position babies pictured in Stanton's *Heubach's Little Characters* on page 13; Negro; Vasser girls with wigs; and babies with molded shifts. Most came in a series of six different poses. It is interesting to note that these were included in the doll section of the catalog which seems to indicate that they were also intended as playthings for children, not simply for ornamentation.

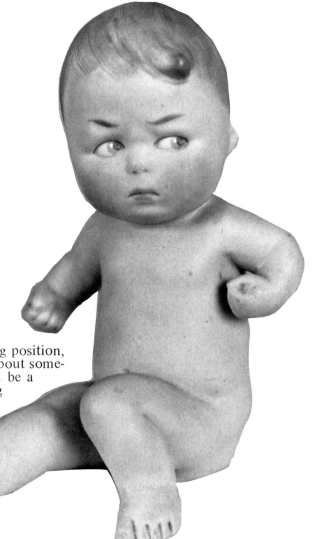

Illustration 108. This fellow, 5in (12.7cm) tall in a sitting position, carries the square mark with 9744. He is certainly angry about something. A look at his companion in Illustration 109 might be a clue. Someone ate all of his cake! There is no molding detail in the hair except for a tiny curl on the side of his forehead, but the painting is nicely done with brush strokes indicating strands of hair. Frown ridges are molded above his eyes, and the eyebrows show careful treatment. His mouth with the turned down edges contributes to his pouty look. The ears are very small, almost an afterthought. *Richard Wright Collection.*

Illustration 109. Here is the same angry fellow shown in Illustration 108 with a contented-looking buddy, hands on his tummy in obvious satisfaction, mouth upturned in a smug expression, eyes squinty from his smile, almost cross-eyed really. Like his pal, his hair has no detail except for a curl at the center top of his head. He has a vase attached to his back, so was intended for some practical purpose. He is incised with a square mark and 9855. *Richard Wright Collection.*

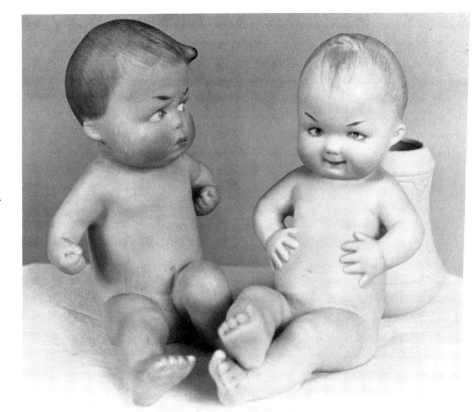

Illustration 111. The workmanship of this 3½in (8.9cm) fellow is definitely not up to Heubach standards. He would have been overlooked except that he was recognized as being in a known Heubach position and when he was lifted up, sure enough, there was his square mark and 9202. His hair is plain with a top curl. Neither hair, eyebrows, eyes, nor mouth is well painted. But he does have an appealing expression. Is he expecting us to guess what is hidden in his cupped hand? Some creepy, crawling thing, I am sure! *Richard Wright Collection.*

Illustration 110. Although unmarked, this boy is obviously another example of the boy in Illustration 109 showing that Heubach often used the same form either by itself or with a vase or box attached. However, this boy seems to have been painted by a different artist, and the overall effect is not so striking. The eyes are less dramatic, the mouth is less pronounced, and the paint strokes on the head are further apart. However, there is excellent molding on the toes, even showing the toenails. *Mackemull Collection.*

Action Figures

Heubach made a good variety of these naked figures with molded shoes or boots. Half the fun of these action figures is in imagining the circumstances which provoked their expressions. It is interesting that these children have such realistic poses and faces. Their design must have involved a good deal of work on the part of the artist, including observation of children and the sculpting of them. The facial expressions run the gamut of emotion from pensive to angry, from startled to happy, with excellent modeling detail in the faces and a fair amount in the bodies as well.

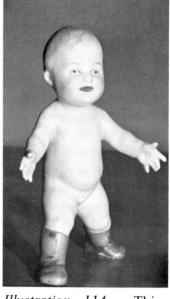

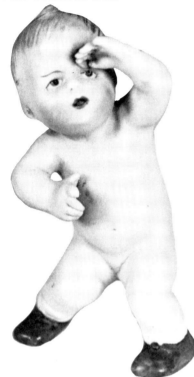

Illustration 112. What could this fellow be seeing? Something in the sky obviously -- maybe even Superman? He is 4in (10.2cm) tall with low brown oxfords and molded white socks. His open/closed mouth has a molded tongue. There is a curl on the top of his head; his hair is brush-stroked on. An unusual treatment was given to his eyebrows; the waviness gives him a frown. He is incised with a square mark and 0210, which maybe should have a 1 in front of it which did not print. *Richard Wright Collection.*

Illustration 114. This boy, 6½in (16.5cm) tall, is a slightly larger version of the boy in Illustration 113 shown here again by himself for a clearer view. He is of exceptionally fine bisque, nicely tinted with excellent molding detail. The quality of this figure is much better than the one in Illustration 113. He has a molded curl on his forehead and beautifully colored hair. The chubby legs and arms with typical Heubach fingers make him look like a healthy fellow indeed. His brown boots come just below his dimpled knee. Neither boy is marked, but both have definite Heubach characteristics. *H&J Foulke.*

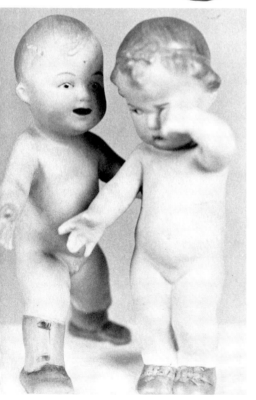

Illustration 113. The boy is imploring the girl not to cry anymore. Did he break her favorite doll? Whatever happened, she is certainly unhappy! Her molded hair is done in a sweet style, smooth on the crown and curled below her orange hair band tied in the front. She has the typical Heubach hand. Her shoes are brown with molded bows in front; her low socks are white. She is 6in (15.2cm) tall, and is incised with the square mark and 10056. *Both Richard Wright Collection.*

Illustration 115. Such a shy fellow he is as he holds his bouquet of flowers. Maybe he is thinking of presenting them to the crying girl! Apparently of the same series as the boy in Illustration 114, he has the same brown boots coming up to his knee. He is attached to a vase. Both vase and one shoe carry a square mark. The other shoe is impressed 10055. He is also 6½in (16.5cm) tall. *Richard Wright Collection.*

Easter Bunnies

Next to Christmas, Easter is probably the holiday which offers the greatest opportunity for appealing novelties. All kinds of possibilities present themselves with children, bunnies and chicks. Apparently the Heubach factory was attuned to consumers and overlooked few opportunities to create a product to fill any possible gap or to create an object to market with a seasonal theme.

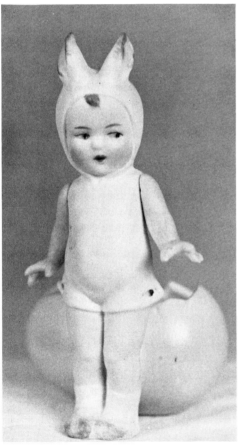

Illustration 117. The 5½in (14.0cm) companion bunny girl looks just a bit uncertain as she stands in front of her attached pink egg. Her delicately pink tinted ears are shorter than the boy's, and a tiny lock of hair peeks out from under her cap. Her bunny costume stops in a short skirt with holes into the bisque on both sides for insertion of a prettily tied ribbon. Her jointed arms are flesh-colored with hands outstretched in a pert attitude. She is incised 10540 with a square mark. *Richard Wright Collection.*

Illustration 116. This 6in (15.2cm) boy in a bunny costume was doubtless intended as an Easter novelty. The attached egg would hold tiny Easter candies. His flesh-tinted face is sweetly flirtatious with side-glancing eyes and a mischievous watermelon mouth. The molded rabbit suit is white with yellow tinted shading at the ears. His egg is pale yellow. Oddly enough, his suit is apparently sleeveless, as the jointed arms are flesh-tinted with no indication of a molded sleeve. He is incised 10539 with a square mark. *Richard Wright Collection.*

Black Position Babies

Black items were popular novelties in the last quarter of the 19th and first quarter of the 20th centuries. Apparently they were consistent sellers as a few figures and dolls were always included in the catalogs of the period. However, judging from the difficulty of finding these old Negro items today, they were not overwhelming best sellers.

The modeling in the black figures created by the Brothers Heubach was done with great care and attention to realistic detail. The hair was given a fuzzy look by the application of tiny bisque particles, certainly a time-consuming step in producing the babies. The eyes were deeply incised with even the eyelids being carefully molded. Distinctive Negroid features include the broad noses and wide lips. Some of the figures have the sunburst mark; on others it was omitted.

These are the only figures that carry the impressed COPYRIGHTED within two circles mark. It has been suggested by Richard Wright that these figures might be based on the "Coon Calendar" for 1900 which was copyrighted in 1899 by H. Reck.

Illustration 118. The largest of this group of four figures is 5in (12.7cm) tall. He is clutching a cob of corn as though someone might try to get it away from him. The eye detail on this fellow, which is especially good, is emphasized by interesting eyebrows. His white shift has painted blue dots. Unfortunately, the black tinting on the body and hair does not wear well and often white spots show through. *Richard Wright Collection.*

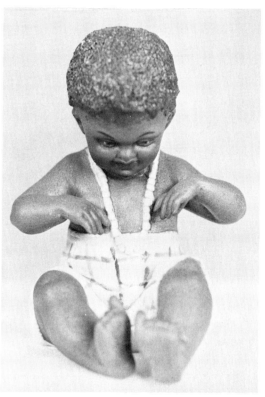

Illustration 119. This 4½in (11.5cm) fellow, wearing a molded blue necklace, seems absorbed in wiggling his two big toes which are given special definition. Again the facial modeling is excellent with emphasis on detail around his broad nose and mouth. His trousers are white with painted crossing stripes for decoration. *Richard Wright Collection.*

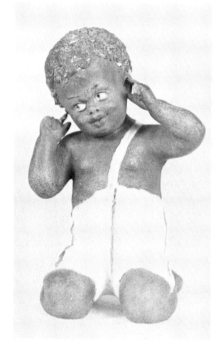

Illustration 120. The kneeling boy is 4in (10.2cm) tall, designed with fingers pointing to his ears. Perhaps the boy in the next illustration is saying things he does not want to hear! His face does not look disturbed, however, as it has a somewhat quizzical expression emphasized by the whites of his eyes which stand out on the black face. All of the detail on him is well executed with particular attention to the fingers. His white trousers with only one strap are decorated with stripes. *Richard Wright Collection.*

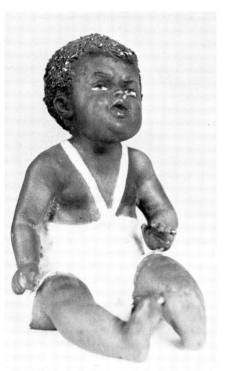

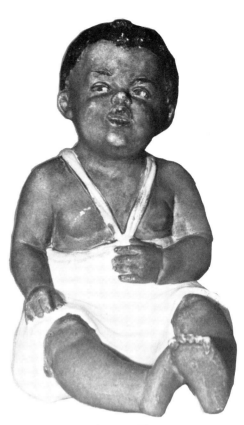

Illustration 121. This 4½in (11.5cm) boy in the V-strapped romper with turquoise polka dots certainly looks concerned about something. In fact, he is almost scowling. He has molded frown lines above his eyebrows; his eyes are partially closed with heavy lids. His mouth is partially open with two tiny white teeth showing, as though he is ready to complain. Even one hand is clenched. *Richard Wright Collection.*

Illustration 122. Here is nearly the same baby as in Illustration 121 in a larger size. At first glance, he is the same, but closer examination shows subtle differences. He does not appear to be frowning as fiercely, and his eyes are side-glancing. Instead of being free, his arms are molded onto his body. His shift does not have the painted spots. Perhaps this was a later version of the previous doll. He is 5½in (14.0cm) tall. *Mackemull Collection.*

ABOVE: Illustration 123. This egg is a very rare Heubach item, indeed. Probably made as an Easter novelty, it carries the incised sunburst mark. The egg is held by one small black boy and three little black heads and one pair of arms are breaking through the shell. The egg is 5in (12.4cm) tall. Babies breaking through eggs was a popular theme for novelties of the period. These are several bisque versions of a white baby coming from an egg, as well as a lovely one done in wax. *Mackemull Collection.*

RIGHT: Illustration 124. This small 3in (7.6cm) black boy playing the accordian is dressed in a clown suit. Though unmarked, he is possibly a Heubach figure as he has some similarity to the other figures. His hair has good molding to give it a natural look. He was possibly one of a set of musicians. *Mackemull Collection.*

Piano Babies

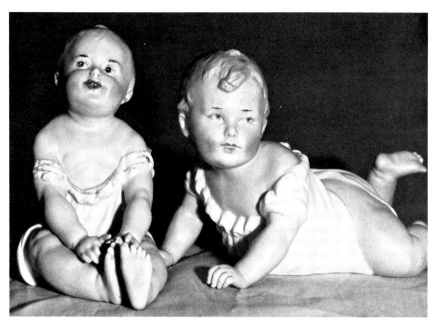

Heubach ornamental piano babies are outstanding among the bisque figures created by the millions in the porcelain factories of Germany during the late Victorian period, the last quarter of the 19th century. There is always controversy among collectors about which came first, dolls or figures. I personally feel that the figurines came first and were the inspiration for the character dolls which came at the turn of the 20th century. Certainly a connection cannot be denied as it is easy to see family likenesses in the faces of the dolls and figures. Sometimes even the same face occurs as a figurine and as a doll. The piano babies by Heubach are outstanding because of their realistic looks and natural poses. The models were obviously done from real life, and attention was given to all of the details necessary to make the babies look alive, including toes, fingers, fat rolls, dimples, intaglio eyes and molded natural-looking hair.

Illustration 125. The baby on the left, although losing his nightgown which is trimmed with tiny beads of paint, looks happy as he reaches for his toes, a favorite preoccupation with barefooted children. He is 5in (12.7cm) tall and has the incised sunburst mark. Even among Heubach-designed babies he is outstanding for the realistic modeling in his body, arms and legs. It is easy enough to see his well-fed look with fat rolls at his ankles and wrists, as well as dimpled elbows and knees. His intaglio eyes with raised white highlights look to the side, and he has two tiny upper teeth. The crawling baby on the right is 7in (17.8cm) long and has the incised sunburst mark with 3101. His outstanding feature is his beautiful blonde hair so exquisitely molded with locks of curls on his forehead and above his ears with overall comb marks to give real texture. His white shift is trimmed with an aqua bow. *Mackemull Collection.*

Illustration 126. The baby on the left is 6in (15.2cm) long. She is a frequently found bisque figure which came in many sizes from about 4in (10.2cm) to 12in (30.5cm). Her most outstanding feature is her molded bonnet which is done in a crocheted-type style. A molded green ribbon is threaded through the cap and ties at the top. Wisps of blonde hair peek out from under the edges of the cap. The neck and sleeves of the shift are trimmed with a molded ruffle and raised paint dots. Her open/closed mouth has two tiny white upper teeth. This baby can also be found without the bonnet, perhaps intended as a boy. The crawling baby on the right shows a family resemblance to his companion. He is just 4¼in (10.9cm) long. Both figures are marked with a sunburst. *Mackemull Collection.*

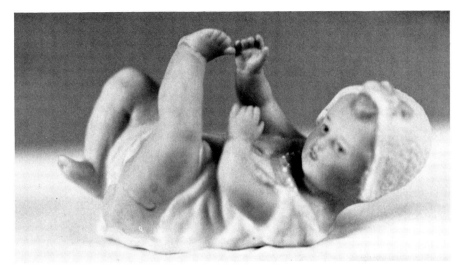

Illustration 127. This 4½in (11.5cm) long size also has a sunburst mark. Her chemise and bonnet are trimmed with blue bows. The arms and legs show almost no fat rolls; the eyes do not have much life; the cap is not very detailed and does not have a ribbon entwined around the brim. *Ruth Noden Collection.*

Illustration 128. These two children are a part of a small but interesting and unusual Heubach item, just 4½in (11.5cm) tall with green-stamped sunburst mark and 5965. The other part of the trio is a piglet! All three seem contented, even the pig. The children are nicely modeled and show a family resemblance to faces on other figurines. The soft coloring is also typically Heubach. *H&J Foulke.*

Illustration 129. A larger version of the baby in Illustration 126, this one is 9in (22.9cm) long and also has the sunburst mark. The larger size has much more detail in the modeling - - particularly on the bonnet and in the eyes and mouth. Also the fingers are much more distinctive. The eyes and the mouth have been much more carefully painted. The shading on the lips is especially nice. *Richard Wright Collection.*

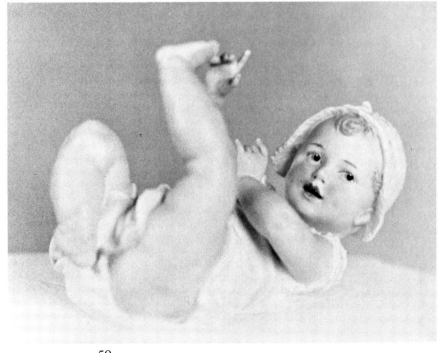

A Collector's Delight

Illustration 130A, B & C. One of the most spectacular Heubach pieces with babies is this bisque basket trinket box with a removable lid. The woven basket is tinted a natural straw color with the top edge, basket rim and clasps and hinges in a darker brown. Four blonde haired babies peek over the rim of the basket. All of the babies have the most realistic expressions with very detailed modeling. This certainly must have been a costly item to produce as the intricate detail is simply astounding. The baby on the left has an open/closed mouth with shading on his lower lip and two molded upper teeth. His eyes are dark and deeply incised. His hands are molded into clenched fists with very detailed fingers. The girl in the center has a molded fabric bonnet surrounded by a ruffle and covered with pink polka dots. A bow ties under her chin. Her lips and eyes are outstanding. The hand which rests on the hamper rim is done in typical Heubach style. The center boy has his elbow resting on the basket; his hair and hands are beautifully modeled. In the right corner is another little girl in a molded white cap. She looks a little younger than the middle girl. She has just one curl exposed under her eyelet edged bonnet. Since she does not look as happy as the others, perhaps she is feeling a little crowded with all of those larger babies in such a small basket! This rare and exquisite piece has been coveted by many Heubach collectors. The basket measures 8½in (21.6cm) long and 7in (17.8cm) high; it is marked with a sunburst. *Ruth Noden Collection.*

Flower Children

Absolutely amazing for the amount of minute detail involved in the making are these two children with large floppy hats, or what at first glance appear to be sunbonnets. However, when these are viewed from the back, they are actually inverted flowers; hence, these will be called the "flower children."

Illustration 131. The face of this baby is unbelievable for a figurine. The eyes are deeply incised and very lifelike. The eyeball is molded as well as the upper and lower eyelids; the eyebrows are not only molded, but are beautifully feathered by the artist. The open/closed mouth gives her the illusion of getting ready to speak. One expects to hear all kinds of satisfied gurgling sounds from her since she has succeeded in pulling off one stocking and has started on the second. The evenly-applied flesh tones give her a natural rosy and healthy complexion. Her dress is white with pink trim and polka dots; her hat is also pink and white. She is 10½in (26.7cm) tall and is stamped in blue with the sunburst mark. *Ruth Noden Collection.*

Illustration 132. An older sister of the flower baby shown in Illustration 131, the face of this little girl shows the family resemblance. She is shy, but has been caught in this tiny glance upward which may have lasted for only a few seconds at most. Her eyes are done with as much care as was lavished on the baby, but they are not as wide open, befitting her mood. Her lips are closed but give a hint of just the beginning of a smile which may be coaxed into full bloom. What a reward for the lucky recipient! Again this flower girl has the bloom of health in her rosy skin tones. As is appropriate for an older child, she is wearing a dress in a more streamlined style which hangs gracefully from a high waistline. Her dress is trimmed with turquoise as is her bonnet and she is wearing shoes and stockings. This young girl is also 10½in (26.7cm) tall, and paired with the flower baby, the two make a breathtaking impression. As with other Heubach figures, these flower children have been seen in a smaller size which, while lovely, do not have as much detail as the larger models. *Ruth Noden Collection.*

Child Figurines

Heubach was a prolific producer of not only dolls, but also figurines. Here is a presentation of some of the child figures since they are the most interesting to collectors of dolls. Most doll collectors do include a number of these child figures among their doll display since they are charming, appealing and eye-catching. Figurines were popular mantelpiece and table ornaments in the Victorian period and were carried over into the 20th century. They are difficult to date as the molds, which were expensive to produce in the first place, were undoubtedly used for long periods of time, just as with dolls. The word "Germany" had to be used on all articles for export after 1891, and does provide a dividing date of sorts. However, many times the "Made in Germany" was simply stamped on the bottom of a piece and just as easily wore off, or was possibly washed off, as bisque figures which sit out on tables or shelves exposed to the air collect a lot of dust and real dirt which makes washing them in soap and water necessary.

After becoming familiar with the Heubach style, one can almost always spot a Heubach figure, even before looking at the identifying mark. The faces always show real expressions and emotions as well as family resemblances. The clothing with frills and ruffles has fabric as well as sewing detail. The hair is usually blonde; the eyes are usually blue as one would expect of a Teutonic child anyway. The coloring of the figure is very soft. Many times a garment is left white, with color being used only for the trim of ribbons, polka dots, stripes and similar details.

Illustration 134. This little girl shows the piety expected of Victorian children who were supposed to be restrained in their manner. Anyway, it is difficult for people to resist a child who looks as angelic as this one. Perhaps she has seen the first star of the evening and is sending up her wish prayer. Her nightgown has a blue yoke and is trimmed with the gold often found on Heubach figures. She is 8in (20.3cm) tall and marked with a red-stamped sunburst. A companion piece to this one is a slightly older girl with long blonde hair, hands with fingertips together and full instead of cuffed sleeves. *Ruth Noden Collection.*

Illustration 135. This cheeky fellow is not only playing at soldier, he is taking himself very seriously about the task as he smokes on his wooden cigar. In full military dress including a sword at his side and boots, he is propped up against an attached vase in an almost "What do you think of me" attitude. This is an unusual figure. He is 5½in (14.0cm) tall and has the incised sunburst mark. *Mackemull Collection.*

Illustration 136. Many of the Heubach figures were made in pairs or series, and this fellow is half of a boy-girl pair. Leaning on his elbows, chin in hand, he has a most appealing and flirtatious look on his face. His smiling mouth has a very wide lower lip and molded teeth. His dark eyes are narrowed and side-glancing, but are deeply incised. His blouse is white with a pink collar, cuffs and polka dots. He is 6½in (16.5cm) tall and has the stamped sunburst mark. *Mackemull Collection.*

LEFT: Illustration 137. This 13in (33.0cm) figure of a girl with a dove is an example of one of the most idealistic figures produced by Heubach. It is certainly lovely, but does not seem to have as much realism as most of their other figures. The girl's hair is especially well done in a slightly different style, pulled back with a turquoise bow. Her shift has turquoise shading and tiny handpainted flower decorations. Two more realistic details appear, though, in the chubby dimpled knees and the stockings, one up and one down! *Richard Wright Collection.*

RIGHT: Illustration 138. A favorite with doll collectors is this little girl holding her doll, as many of them also like figures and pictures of children with dolls. She is 10in (25.4cm) tall and carries a red sunburst mark. Sitting on an upturned basket with feet gripping the sides for balance, she is the picture of a real little girl possibly admonishing the doll to go to sleep. Certainly, she is very serious about her task, judging from the concentration shown in her face. Her blonde hair has bangs which are gently pushed to one side and braids over and behind her shoulders. Her blue crocheted jumper and rose tam contrast with her white ruffled blouse. Her doll, which in real life would perhaps be a bisque shoulder head on a kid body, also has long blonde flowing hair, stiff arms and a lovely yellow dress with white ruffle trim which appears to be a baby dress. *Ruth Noden Collection.*

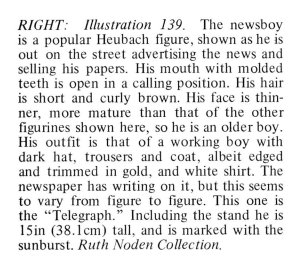

RIGHT: Illustration 139. The newsboy is a popular Heubach figure, shown as he is out on the street advertising the news and selling his papers. His mouth with molded teeth is open in a calling position. His hair is short and curly brown. His face is thinner, more mature than that of the other figurines shown here, so he is an older boy. His outfit is that of a working boy with dark hat, trousers and coat, albeit edged and trimmed in gold, and white shirt. The newspaper has writing on it, but this seems to vary from figure to figure. This one is the "Telegraph." Including the stand he is 15in (38.1cm) tall, and is marked with the sunburst. *Ruth Noden Collection.*

ABOVE: Illustration 140. This 17in (43.2cm) dandy in full day dress is certainly a high point as far as Heubach figurines are concerned. His face shows that he is looking expectantly from dark side-glancing eyes for approval of his outfit. His mouth is open in expectation of replying to an approving comment. His outfit is certainly spectacular. The top hat and jacket are ivory with gold trim and buttons; his shirt is white with gold studs; his tie is burgundy as is his vest. His wide-bottomed trousers are brown with burgundy stripes. His accessories include an enameled rose in one hand, a walking stick with dog-head handle in the other hand, glasses sitting low on his nose and a fancy handkerchief in his pocket. *Richard Wright Collection.*

Illustration 141. Certainly a rare Heubach figure is this glazed china boy, a real departure from the myriad of bisque items made. He has beautiful molding for such a small figure with good detail in his eyes and hair, as well as the fabric of his sweater. His mouth is open as though whistling, and with hand in pocket, he presents a jaunty look. The coloring is interesting as it is reminiscent of the Royal Copenhagen figurines, gray white with just a hint of color in his pale gray suit and tan shoes. The vase against which he is leaning is like that of the boy with the cigar in Illustration 135. Just 6½in (16.5cm) tall, he is marked with a green stamped square mark, the only item in this book marked in such a way. However, quite a few glazed china animals finished in this same style stamped in the same way have been seen. *Mike White Collection.*

Illustration 142. This acrobatic fellow is a part of a series of boys at various types of play and came in both the large 12in (30.5cm) size as this one, and a smaller size of about 8in (20.3cm). He has a face typical of the Heubach company, a smiling mouth with teeth showing, deep cheek dimples, eyes just glancing up at the viewer as though looking for approval of his stunt. His blue shirt, a hole torn in the sleeve, has white beaded accents; his purple trousers stop at the knee. His position is so real; all of us have seen children acrobatting around like this. The base of the figurine is green and grassy; in the background is what is probably a bush. He is marked with the sunburst as well as the red Made in Germany circle. *Mike White Collection.*

Illustration 143. Heubach figures are known for catching emotions from serious as shown in Illustration 134 to frivolous as this little girl with the powder box in one hand and the puff in another. She flirts with herself in the mirror as she pretends to be very grown-up. Her blonde hair is long and wavy, and her face is older than that of the child in Illustration 134. Her undergarment is trimmed with gold, and the turquoise polka dots are surrounded with tiny raised paint dots, often a Heubach decorative technique, but one which does not usually show up in photographs. Again notice the raised big toe, also often seen on Heubach figures. Behind the girl is an attached vanity stool in dark turquoise. Its lid removes to reveal a trinket box. She is 10in (25.4cm) tall and stamped in blue with the sunburst. *Richard Wright Collection.*